TURN-ONS!

185 Strategies for the Secondary Classroom

Stephen K. Smuin

Fearon Pitman Publishers, Inc.

Belmont, California

To my students

- at San Mateo High School, especially Ellie Freidman and Freddie Rivers
- at Libby Senior High School, especially Janet Nowell, Becky Schultz, Sheila Rose, and my athletes
- at Upward Bound Program, especially Lyda Fast Horse and Tom Stockstill
- and at Loyola-Sacred Heart High School, especially Colleen, Kathy, and Patsy McNamara, Stacy Weldele, Karen Stout, Kathleen Mangan, Keith Giles, Patti Hudson, Mark McQuirk, Mike Norman, Vince Sparacino, and Vickie Spencer.

This book is really yours.

Acknowledgments

I wish also to state my special thanks to James Turner, my first principal, who encouraged my development; to Dean Roberts, who gave me an opportunity; to Royal Barnell, who allowed me class time to do the first organizational work for this book; to Ken Costa, who read the first rough draft; and to my brother Doug, who shaped the second version; to Joan Wolfgang at Fearon Pitman Publishers, Inc., who saw the value of an idea shining through too many pages of writing; to Tom Hollman, who gave me my first chance to teach as I wished; to Dr. Allan Brown, who has been a consistent resource for my personal problem solving and decision making; to my family, of whom I am most definitely a product; and to Moreen, who allowed this book to happen. Thanks, too, to the many other people who contributed directly or indirectly to this book; their efforts have not been forgotten.

Stephen K. Smuin

Edited by Gail Larrick

Designed by Joe di Chiarro

Cover design by Greg Jones

ISBN-0-8224-7051-9

Library of Congress Catalog Card Number: 77-92903

Printed in the United States of America.

1.9 8 7 6 5 4 3 2 1

Contents

Introduction

The lessons of life should determine the students' educational learning plan.

The educational system is returning to the idea that education can no longer take place *only* in school. If the true purpose of education is to prepare students for a good life, then the qualities that constitute a good school should reflect that life. Students must have a choice of what a good life is. School and education must expand out of the four walls of the classroom, beyond the textbooks, and into reality rather than simulation. The school needs to teach the student to function not only in the school environment, but also in all of life's environments.

"What children need, even just to make a living," John Holt writes, "are qualities that can never be trained into a machine—inventiveness, flexibility, resourcefulness, curiosity and above all, judgment." They need to learn self-diagnosis, self-prescription, and self-evaluation. Desirable educational objectives can no longer be defined in terms of ground to be covered. William Glasser has categorized three separate areas in which students need to be taught: education, or the ability to answer questions; thinking, or finding out what to do when you don't know what to do; and learning, or skills such as spelling, reading, math.

How does one develop a method that will make the learning happen? In this book I suggest not a compromise among old methods, but a new approach.

Needed first and foremost is a teacher willing to grow, change, plan, and experience in order to bring about an honest, warm classroom where creative, worthwhile learning can take place. Second, this teacher must open up new areas for interaction between his or her knowledge and the student's quest for knowledge. The strategies in this book are designed to help you do just that. They will help you discover new dimensions of active involvement with your students—teaching, counseling, facilitating. And involvement is the major ingredient required. The strategies usually require little else beyond that, except paper and pencil. It's worth remembering that Socrates, one of history's most effective teachers, had no tape recorder, film projector,

1

packaged games, or multi-media lab specialists; often he didn't even have an answer to his students' questions. But *he* was involved and his students *did* learn.

The strategies in this book are designed to help each student develop the following as a direct result of your classroom curriculum:

- ☐ ability to communicate verbally
- ☐ ability to communicate in writing
- ☐ ability to read a book
- ☐ ability to conduct research
- ☐ ability to make a rational decision
- ☐ awareness of career alternatives
- ☐ knowledge of one's capabilities, abilities, aptitudes, interests in life, and career potential
- ☐ knowledge of the place of one's American and ethnic culture in today's world culture
- ☐ knowledge of how and why one is a product of history
- ☐ ability to study effectively
- ☐ understanding and appreciation of the humanities that will lead to involvement in the arts
- ☐ sense of the importance and place of science
- ☐ awareness of one's body and how to utilize, develop, and maintain a healthy, active body
- ☐ a trusting relationship with at least one faculty member
- ☐ achievement of or progress toward a positive self-image and a sense of self-worth
- ☐ ability to maintain oneself and to prosper in today's economic, social, and legal/financial society
- ☐ understanding of the structure and ramifications of American politics in the national and international arenas
- ☐ ability to have fun while learning

I have used the techniques in this book in courses in world history, American history, social science, sociology, psychology, American government, social psychology, and economics and in such diverse settings as parochial and ghetto schools, federal Indian programs, Elementary and Secondary Education Act projects, and special innovative education programs, as well as in substitute-teaching situations.

No person works in a vacuum. In developing the many original strategies in this book, I have drawn ideas from ballet, sports, literature, television commercials, newspaper stories, and everyday life experiences. I have observed many teachers, and I have borrowed and traded strategies; I have modified strategies suggested by others so that they apply to social studies. Exercises have been sent to me. A few strategies have been taken from college methods courses. Some of the exercises are old ethnic games; some have been used so often that no amount of research could determine their original sources.

The strategies can be used to introduce or further a theme, to stimulate the real functioning of a theme, or to debrief past study. They *cannot* be used *in place of* fundamental educational data on the topics themselves. They serve to supplement and provide motivation for a well-constructed educational plan, not to substitute for the plan. Often background information, case studies, material from the text, or other data must be examined before, during, or after these strategies.

While the strategies are arranged in a developmental order based upon their actual classroom use, most of them can be adapted for use in several curriculum areas, and users should feel free to create their own sequence.

An important note: These strategies were not written or collected with the idea that teachers will use them to do psychological work-ups on students; they are *not* intended as encounter-group exercises. All of the strategies are nonthreatening and are based on positive feedback. At first, students may show some embarrassment at the new techniques, but your handling of the situation and the example of your participation should quickly change this response to interaction. Most important, the positive results that students find themselves achieving will eliminate their doubts.

Your role, however, must go beyond participation. You must ask these important questions before and after the use of each strategy: What did the strategy prove, teach, clarify, or introduce? How does the strategy apply to what we are studying in class? How does it apply to your lives?

This book is written primarily for classroom teachers. It will also be valuable to prospective teachers, to substitute teachers looking for ideas, for use in college methods courses in education, and as a basis for schools' in-service programs.

S.K.S.

Class Starters

The basis for all the strategies contained in this book is interaction. For these strategies to be effective, you, the teacher, must be an effective facilitator of these interactions. Section 1 of this unit explores the philosophy of sound interaction techniques and presents practical suggestions for improving the quality of classroom discussion, role playing, simulation, and inquiry. You may wish to share some of this material with your students so that they may understand some of the finer points of carrying on productive interactions.

Section 2, Building Classroom Structure, offers suggestions for changing the physical, emotional, and operating environment of the classroom. The strategies run the gamut from the introduction of a student journal to the building of study carrels. The goal of this group of strategies is to develop humanistic practices within the classroom.

Section 3, Development of Group Concept, suggests strategies for developing the class into a sensitive, caring, one-for-all-and-all-for-one group. The strategies are not all subject oriented; their goal is to bring thirty individuals together as a group through shared experiences. The strategies range from making name tags to activities that develop trust among group members.

The final section, Group Concept at Work, puts the class to work as a developed group; mutually, class members learn to solve problems, answer questions, and determine ways to function effectively as a group. Cooperation and problem-solving and decision-making skills are stressed in Section 4.

1 Interaction Techniques

The four major interaction techniques are role playing, simulation, inquiry, and discussion.

Role playing is the exercise of playing out another person's role, forcing the actor to learn how others feel, react, and make decisions. Role playing is usually open-ended.

Simulations are prescribed role playings, exercises that attempt to approximate real-life situations through the carrying out of representative roles in which the players make responses and decisions based on real-life examples. Those who assume the roles reap the rewards and suffer the consequences of their decisions in the final outcome of the simulation. The simulation is then debriefed and analyzed by and for the students. (Throughout this book, the term *debrief* is used to define the process of examining through discussion or other means what took place during the performance of a strategy, why it took place, and what has been learned by participation in the strategy.)

Simulations are active rather than passive learning situations. Simulations generally do more than teach information, since they are primarily concerned with using information to make decisions, solve problems, and answer questions. To be effective, simulations usually must have an interdisciplinary approach.

While students respond most freely to competitive simulations and enjoy them most, the assignments, debriefings, and evaluations must emphasize *how* someone won and *what* each person learned, rather than *who* won. Winning is not the goal of a simulation. Learning *how* to win and absorbing the basic material presented *is* its goal.

I have included some strategies that take the student beyond the simulation stage to real-life rather than life-like experiences. Patti Lou Shultz and Lance Dublin define this process as "experiential learning," in their article "Antioch College West," in Marcia Perlstein's *Flowers Can Even Bloom in Schools.* As you prepare to present material to your students, ask yourself how you could involve them in discovering the material and making use of it in daily life. As you consider that problem, you are on the way to developing experiential learning as a facet of your program.

Inquiry, or the discovery method, is simply a mental search from point A to point Z of a subject. If you were to use the inquiry method in a mountain-climbing course, you certainly wouldn't take the class to the base of a high peak and say, "I'll see you at the top." Instead, you and the class would explore together the methods of solving the problems involved in the climb, laying out the alternatives, and doing costs/benefits analysis and research. Once the students had developed skills applicable to mountain climbing, they could develop a plan for climbing the mountain.

Some teachers believe students don't learn because they haven't been presented enough data or the correct data. But more often the problem is that they don't know what data are or what a particular item means. Students must be taught to identify and analyze data, to be critical thinkers and synthesizers. The skills they learn can then be applied to any type of data.

How much must the teacher lead in inquiry? How much background material must the student have before being left on his or her own? The answers depend not only on the strategy but on the individual goals of that strategy. The smaller the task, the further removed it is from your final goal, the less leading you need to do. If you use a developmental approach, each step will present a small, manageable component to the students. With each incremental step the student solves, he or she is more prepared to solve the next step alone. Whenever possible, stay out of the problem-solving discussions.

Once students understand the process of inquiry, they can apply it to any problem. Though you start with a goal (acquiring mountain-climbing skills), you don't preplan the application of their problem-solving skills. (Your students may choose to explore the back trail, take up rock climbing, or even forget the whole thing!) A teacher who has predetermined the outcome of a discovery session will consciously or unconsciously direct the inquiry toward that "goal."

In essence, to conduct inquiry you must function as a social scientist. You must develop the idea that students are not *studying* history but, rather, *creating* history; they are not learning sociology but are functioning as sociologists.

The first step in the process of inquiry is to develop objectives. Are you attempting to identify a problem, find a solution, answer a question, satisfy a curiosity, clarify some values, resolve a value conflict, determine the validity of a generalization, or gather relevant data about an issue? An objective may be established in one of two ways: You may examine your data and determine your objective, or you may determine your objective and then seek the relevant data. While some steps in the inquiry process will always be similar, once you establish the specific objective, much of the methodology will be predetermined.

The major problem in high school inquiry is that students do not stay on task. This problem generally arises when the class has not clearly defined its task. Once the task is defined to the satisfaction of the group, the method of proceeding will become clear. Next, in a brain-storming session (see Strategy 9), the task should be broken down into its smallest components on the blackboard. Once the components are defined, committees may work effectively with each small unit, with the larger group approving each committee recommendation. When the sequence of necessary steps has been established, the class can begin developing tentative approaches to each step, analyzing alternatives, defining the costs/benefits of each and finally choosing a rational answer or course of action.

Having shared this process with the students, you are now prepared to guide them in data collection and verification. At this point, the students are already involved in the process of inquiry. Many have emotional, vested interests in solutions they have helped to clarify. Thus they are more willing to accept the challenge of doing pure research.

Discussion is any open-ended verbal interaction between members of the class (including the teacher). It need not be a debate or problem-solving session. Basically the goal is to allow members of the class to make known their views and perhaps ask questions. There is no predetermined concluding objective.

Remember that facilitating a discussion is not the same as directing a group toward arrival at the "right answer." It is more desirable for you to maintain a supportive role than a directive role in discussions. Help students when they are groping, but don't grope for them. Clarify only the questions they want clarified; don't be the sort of discussion leader who constantly restates the response in better language. But just as you should not dominate the discussion, neither should a small group of students. Involve everyone in the exchange. Watch for signs that a student is interested in getting into the conversation, then quickly call on that student. Look at the students, nod as they speak; you must reinforce their behavior if you want it to continue.

Some students may have trouble expressing themselves. When you hear someone say, "I don't know how to put it," encourage the student to continue talking; offer to interpret. Remember a wrong answer is better than no answer at all, as it may open more doors than a right answer. One dynamic teacher explained her technique for involving students who didn't know the answer to a question. Each student who didn't know the answer was invited to choose someone to help discover the answer. The method developed helping relationships and completely stopped students from laughing at others.

You need to instill the idea that students need to get involved. As you become acquainted with the students in your class, you'll learn which students are always ready with the right answer and which are less sure of themselves. Start the shy ones out with simple "yes" or "no" questions. Get them on stage and off stage quickly, with positive results. Small successes will lead to more self-confidence and a willingness to get involved in discussions.

The Harvard Social Studies Project is the basis for some guidelines for discussion as it applies to the conduct of inquiry:

> Fruitful discussion has to be more than a debate, and it has to be more than an occasion to defend views. A combative posture will not result in true inquiry. Students should be encouraged to think of discussion as an opportunity to develop and clarify their views.
>
> Help students to understand that changing their minds is not a mark of inferiority, but a sign of maturity. Students must be sensitive to new evidence and valid reasoning.
>
> Discourage the notion that all opinions are equally valid. Insist that the class establish objective standards for judging the rationality and validity of their positions. Impress upon students the idea that some opinions are better than others.
>
> Prepare students to have a questioning attitude when the "facts" are presented in a discussion. Facts have many interpretations. Source of information must be considered and value judgments must be made. Discussion is not just talking.
>
> Students must be encouraged in a discussion to use their sense of intuition. Guesses are a must along with playing hunches. Encourage students to vocalize random ideas so that the group may bring order and meaning to the randomness.[1]

The skills of interaction are multifaceted. They include: skills in intellectual organization; collection of basic data; management; and verification; as well as the verbal skills used in successful role playings, simulations, inquiries, and discussions. But to what does one apply these newfound skills? In your classroom, you can help students apply them to the strategies contained in this book. Then your students, having practiced these skills, should be able to apply them to the everyday situations of living.

---

[1] As reproduced in a workshop handout received by the author.

2 Building Classroom Structure

1 JOURNAL WRITING

The strategies in this book serve as a means of developing lines of communication—one way to assure an open, honest, and creative classroom. The use of the intensive journal is an effective way to promote communication. Journal writing offers students an opportunity for self-expression and allows you, the teacher, to keep abreast of the effectiveness of the strategies you introduce and to measure the growth of your students. Your written responses to journal notations offer you a form of direct communication with each student.

Ask each student to acquire a six-by-nine-inch spiral notebook with three section dividers, labeled "Notes," "Journal Notations," and "My Eyes Only." The journals are never graded. Merely record whether they have been written in.

What kinds of things go into the journal? Generally speaking, anything the student wishes to include. Some students will draw pictures, write poems, or staple articles onto the pages. Many will respond to occurrences, experiences, and happenings in the classroom. You may present the students quotes to which they may respond. The sooner they realize the journal is their own and not homework, the sooner their entries and your responses will allow you both to communicate. Do not expect from your students anything that you are not willing to give yourself. Most important, assure, reassure, and demonstrate that you honor the confidential nature of the journal.

You may wish to give periodic journal-writing assignments, but students may, and usually do, write in their journals as often as they wish. As the year goes along, you'll find the students' entries becoming more and more honest and from the heart—especially if you put yourself into your responses. You'll find that students will be writing more and more for you, handing their journals in even when it is not required. Journal comments will often lead to face-to-face conversations that probably would never have taken place without the journals.

The journals may be used most effectively in debriefing after a strategy is completed. Often the best form of debriefing is introspection through writing in the journal rather than oral debriefing in front of the class.

You can ask students to respond generally to an exercise, or you can construct the types of responses you would like. You might, for example, use the journal as a debriefing and self-evaluation tool by asking students to complete one or more of the statements listed below.

Yesterday I learned two things that I didn't realize before . . .
Yesterday I relearned that . . .
Yesterday I felt that . . .
Yesterday I discovered that . . .
Yesterday I was surprised that . . .
Yesterday I realized that . . .
Yesterday I was pleased that I . . .
Yesterday I was disappointed that . . .
Yesterday I liked what _____ did when . . .
Yesterday I disliked what _____ did when . . .

If students are groping to define what they are learning, have them write a few short sentences explaining exactly what they think they have been learning. Have the class discuss each response, then arrive at a consensus about what is being learned. Have the students close their eyes and visualize a situation in which the material could be used or applied outside the class. If they don't come up with any comments and if *your* explanations are not too well received, perhaps the point has been made—the strategies may not have been successful.

After lengthy class sessions on a particular subject, the journal responses can be structured by asking the students to complete sentences such as:

The class failed me because . . .
This class has been of greatest help to me because . . .
I have contributed to the class by . . .
My recommendations for this section next year are . . .

One particularly interesting journal assignment is to ask the students to write down during the first few days of class the five questions that they would like to have your class answer for them. In the middle of the term and again at the end, ask the students to discuss in their journals which questions are being or have been answered, and why, and which ones have not, and why.

For the journal to be an effective tool, it must be used, and *you must respond in it.* At first you may have to structure student responses more than you will toward the end of the term when you will be able to say simply, "Give me about fifteen minutes in your journals on what went on today in class," or "Tell me what is going on in your head these days."

A few quotes, questions, and statements are listed below to suggest methods of stimulating journal entries. This list is not comprehensive but may initiate your thinking and research. Keep a notebook of quotes, statements, or questions that you feel will provoke good journal responses. A few I've used successfully include:

If a man does not keep pace with his companions, perhaps it is because he hears a different drummer. Let him step to the music he hears, however measured and far away. — Henry David Thoreau

The greatest happiness of life is being loved for yourself . . . or, more correctly, being loved in spite of yourself. — Victor Hugo

A journey of a thousand miles begins with a single step. — Chinese proverb

Some men see things as they are and say why? I dream things that never were and say why not? — Edward M. Kennedy in his eulogy for his brother Robert (paraphrasing George Bernard Shaw)

Discuss the world as it is and as it could be.

How can you be true to yourself?

How are you giving of yourself?

Can you be lonely in a crowd?

What is the most important question the human race should answer in the next five years? Why is it important? How should it be answered, and why?

With many of the strategies in this book, I have suggested debriefing questions. You may wish to have the students write a journal response to those questions rather than respond orally.

Create the attitude that the journal is an exchange of letters between you and the student, and the strategy will be most rewarding for both of you.

2   CLASSROOM RESTRUCTURING

What takes place in the classroom is very important, but so is the environment in which it takes place. Below are some suggestions to guide you and your students in structuring the classroom environment so that it more closely approximates a room in which the students are comfortable and so that the classroom itself becomes a source of educational stimulation. Many rewarding Saturday and Sunday afternoons can be spent with your students in redecorating the classroom.

The first thing I add to my classroom is a stereo record player; the students bring in their own records. I play music before and after class and sometimes during simple assignments that require little concentration.

Next, students are encouraged to bring items from their own rooms—posters, signs, plants, fish, hamsters, and other "junk."

We always try to build very simple study carrels, or "time-out" rooms, using plywood or even large cardboard cartons such as those used to pack bicycles, appliances, or some paper products. These units can be soundproofed with egg cartons. Several of these carrels hold all the free information I have acquired from organizations, agencies, and governmental departments, who are most generous about sending pamphlets, magazines, handouts, and other printed materials.

In one carrel, I put a cassette tape recorder. Students can listen to one of the data-type lectures I have put on tape or to a tape from the cassette tape library. The students help build the library by recording events they attend or interviews they conduct and by bringing in purchased tapes. Nonwriters may tape-record their journal entries.

If you are fortunate enough to have access to a video recorder, you can make extensive use of it. My class watches selected television programs and records class sessions for evaluation on the following day. In one corner of the room, we establish a film-viewing room, complete with earphones. Students who are doing research or have free time can look at movies; those who miss a movie or need to review can also use the area for viewing.

Some schools will allow you to paint the walls of the classroom. My students look forward to this part of the project enthusiastically.

We reserve one bulletin board solely for articles. This area contains newspaper clippings, magazine pictures, and important announcements. One permanent section of the board holds any mention in the local or school papers of members of the class. On a table below the board are spread all the newspapers and magazines to which I subscribe.

Finally, we move my desk and files to one corner of the room, put a music lectern at the front of the room, and arrange the desks in a circle. We feel that if we are to be involved in discussion with one another, it is imperative that we can view each other. The space in the middle of the circle is used when we want to sit on the floor or when we need to stand up or pair up for certain activities. Since this space is used so frequently, we carpet it, gathering old and discontinued sample squares from all the carpet stores in town. These patches are merely sewn together and laid on the floor to create a colorful, cheap, and comfortable rug.

When I notice students writing on the desks, I put up a piece of butcher paper that covers the entire door, and dangle a felt-tip pen from a string attached to the door. This sheet becomes our official graffiti board and is changed weekly. It totally eliminates writing on the desks. Students even take to leaving important messages for one another on the sheet.

Redoing the classroom with the students makes it *their* classroom, and they take pride in it. It also gives the students a chance to work together on a project. The new classroom is constantly changing. Plants grow, hamsters breed, fresh graffiti sheets go up, new magazines come in, current articles are tacked on the bulletin board.

3   PARENT/TEACHER COMMUNICATION

One of the first things you can do to open lines of communication with parents is to write them a *first-day-of-school letter*. This letter can outline the basic format of your course and the requirements you will make of their children and will list any materials students will be reading, listening to, or watching. Explain whether your class is an honors class, a basic course, an elective, or the like. Finally, invite the parents to visit your classroom anytime.

Four basic programs may be used to promote effective parent/teacher relationships. Other ideas are suggested in Strategy 142, Generation Gap Night.

Parent/teacher *conferences* at midterm of the first quarter are very effective. If your school doesn't do it, set aside a Saturday on your own and send notices to the parents of all your students, telling them that you will be in your classroom to discuss their children's development. You'll be surprised how many sincerely interested parents will come, bringing questions and problems.

Some schools arrange a *parents' evening,* where parents come to school about 5:30 P.M. and go to each class their child attends, as if following the student's regular class schedule. Class periods are about fifteen minutes long. Generally the teachers offer much the same information that might be sent home in a first-day-of-school letter. The advantage of the evening event is that parents have a chance to visit all the teachers at one time and can ask them questions.

Some schools take this concept a step further by setting aside a Saturday on which both parents and students attend all the classes for the full period. Teachers teach a regular class, trying to involve the parents. Parents can thus keep up with the changes taking place in school and become aware of what students are being exposed to in the classroom.

Your class may publish a *monthly newsletter* to serve as continuing communication among class members and parents, school administration, and other teachers. It might include a schedule of films you are planning to show, mention of any guest speakers you have lined up, notice of any special classes or evening seminars that are planned, and a synopsis of the activities of the previous month. Reviews of field trips or movies seen and notice of students' accomplishments can all be included in the newsletter. The newsletter will encourage its readers to visit your classroom.

Don't merely communicate grades to parents. Make *frequent contact* with them regarding all phases of their child's development—not in a "tell-on-the-student" fashion but with a sincere desire to inform them of a student's progress or slumps. Parents can be your biggest allies if you have developed a proper relationship. A short note, a quick call, an invitation to the classroom, or a personal home visit can go a long way toward enlisting parents' aid in achieving the goals and objectives of the classroom.

4   HOME SEMINARS

Before all major tests, you may wish to hold a home seminar. Sometimes the "home" may be the local pizza parlor; sometimes it may be your own home or that of one of the students.

The format? Cola, pizza, and questions about what the test will cover. Answer all questions, even "Is this on the test?" Reexplain any area that remains unclear to the students. Set two rules: that you will volunteer no information (students must ask specific questions), and that you won't answer the same question twice.

This strategy is a very successful means of allowing students to meet you outside of the four walls of the classroom. It helps greatly in developing lines of communication and brings a more informal atmosphere to the classroom.

5 PRE- AND POST-TESTING IN THE AFFECTIVE DOMAIN

While pre- and post-testing of information is important in evaluating your own effectiveness as a teacher, testing in the affective domain is also important. You may wish to administer affective domain tests at the beginning and end of your course. A list of such tests and their sources is included in the Appendix (page 146).

6 TESTS: COMPETITION

Identify students' fears of tests and their problems in taking tests. Discuss how to overcome these fears and problems. Make a study of how to prepare for tests and how to take them.

Debrief. Are tests a form of competition? Who is the test-taker competing against (the test, other students, entrance standards, oneself)? Is grade competition healthy?

7 TESTING THE TEACHER

Students should be made aware that testing is done for comparative purposes as well as to measure teacher effectiveness and to allow students to determine what they have learned.

Suggest that students write a test for you that will determine your competency to teach them. This strategy will help students realize that writing tests is difficult and that testing exactly what you want to know is sometimes challenging.

8   OBJECTIVE SETTING

Invite students to close their eyes and relax. Ask them to visualize, as positively as possible, the activities, problems, and classes they will face during the school year. Have them visualize overcoming all the problems, enjoying all the activities, and getting good grades in all classes. Spend ten minutes doing this visualization.

Following this mental exercise, have students write down the ten most significant accomplishments that took place within the fantasy, then choose the three most important ones. Ask them to list all the reasons they are presently stopped or hindered from accomplishing these same successes in real life. After identifying what elements will help them reach these goals, have the students develop a plan for accomplishing these items.

Each person's three items are then listed on the board—duplicates are eliminated. The group then agrees upon the three items they find most significant for all class members.

Successful completion of this strategy makes success with all future values-clarification strategies more likely. The strategy helps develop decision-making, values-clarification, and prioritizing skills.

9   BRAINSTORMING TECHNIQUES

Brainstorming as a formal process involves presenting the group with a problem, concept, or question and having each member of the class, in turn, make a response. All responses are recorded—a person who has no response when his or her turn comes should pass. Anyone who wants to insert a response out of turn merely snaps his or her fingers and makes the response. No comment is to be made about the responses. Once all responses have been made, the group then goes back and decides which of the suggested responses they will use for the purposes of discussion.

Less formally, you may want to put three recorders at the board and allow the class to call out responses. Act as facilitator to make sure that all comments are recorded on the board. A final discussion list is selected from the recorded responses.

10   BRAINSTORMING TO DEVELOP CURRICULUM

Try the brainstorming technique with one variation: Students may respond only by asking a question about a particular topic rather than
by making a statement. Ask the students to brainstorm the question
"What do you want to know?" Students may respond only by stating
questions. Write their questions on the board. You may use the list of
questions to develop the curriculum for the rest of the course or as the
basis for class discussions, assignments, research, lectures, oral
reports, projects, and so on. Below is a list of questions asked by my
junior and senior students several years ago.

Is God dead, or is the structural church dead?
How can each individual realize his or her full potential?
How is motivation related to realizing one's full potential?
Is one's potential limited?
Is your potential affected by society?
Why do we live?
What is sanity, and what is insanity?
Why did people create societies?
Does proof of reincarnation exist?
Why do people kill?
Does pornography have an adverse effect on people?
Must pornography always be sexual?
Is violence pornographic?
What is yoga?
What are the pros and cons of birth control?
Can one be happy all one's life?
Why do people make war?
Is America really free?
Why can't people get along?
Why do we have a limited amount of fun?
Why do so many young people die?
What is hatred, and why do we experience it?
Why are people condemned for their past?
Why do we have prejudice?
How does one become and stay happy?
What is real?
Have moral standards gone down?
How can we get along with our parents?
How did we get involved in Viet Nam?
Who is to say what is right or wrong?
What is witchcraft?

Is abortion a good means of birth control?
What are the pros and cons of premarital sex?
What is the Warren Report?
Who was Sigmund Freud and what were his ideas?
Who was Karl Marx and what were his ideas?
Who was Adolph Hitler and what were his ideas?
Why is time so important?
What causes homosexuality?
Why is marriage looked upon as a virtue?
Do you show your personality through artistic expression?
Could we live under a one-world government?
What is hypnosis?
What is the place of athletics in today's society?
How can school be made more relevant?
What is socialism?
What are the lessons of history?
Why am I the way I am?
What is history?
Is astrology accurate?
Is it wrong to be different?
Where am I going?
Why do people commit suicide?
What is "Black Politics"?
What is "American-style capitalism"?
What is Communism?
What are the causes and outcomes of revolution?
What is diplomacy?
What is the "cold war"?
What are dreams, and what do they mean?

The above questions, stated just as they were developed by juniors and seniors, reflect what those students wanted to know. Such questions may be answered or further refined by a presentation by a class member. If no one student chooses to delve into a question, you may want to make a presentation pursuing it. The presentations may be both academic in nature and discussion oriented. Students feel that a curriculum based on their own questions is truly theirs, designed to meet their needs.

Debrief. At the end of the brainstorming session, go over the questions. Are the questions rational? Do they include implied assumptions? Are they really statements disguised as questions? Would answering the questions help solve the problems they represent?

3 Development of Group Concept

11 BIOGRAPHICAL CARDS

On the first day of class, even before reading the roll, hand out a five-by-eight-inch index card to each of the students. Ask them to write their names in the left-hand corner and their class period and phone numbers in the right-hand corner. (Give them your number when you introduce yourself.)

Next ask the students to write five statements about themselves, describing their hopes, dreams, fears, hobbies, likes, and dislikes. Assure them that you alone will see the cards, and ask them to be open and honest. Don't expect the students to reveal deeply personal information on the first day. Use the cards in reading the roll during the first week of the term so that you can associate names with faces and statements.

Then put the cards away so that you can give them back on the last day of class—when the students will laugh with surprise at what they wrote!

12 VALUABLE QUESTIONS

You can easily get students to give you "right answers" to your questions; to develop interesting, important, useful, and far-reaching questions is more difficult. John Holt, respected author of *Why Children Fail, Why Children Learn,* and *What Do I Do Monday?* poses these provocative questions in his new book, *Instead of Education:* "What does it mean to say 'two things happen at the same time'?" and "What would it be like to ride through space on the front of a beam of light? What would you see?"

Ask your class the two questions. Don't discuss the *answers* to the questions, but discuss instead whether or not the questions are important and why. Finally, tell your students that Albert Einstein asked himself these questions as a small boy, and they led to his theory of relativity.

13   DISCUSSION STARTERS

You may involve students in positive and engaging classroom discussions by helping them to observe their own responses, as in this exercise, which is based in part on John Holt's "In the Mind Practice" from *Instead of Education.*

Initiate a discussion. After two or three people have spoken, ask the students to think about how they would respond to what has been said thus far. Ask them to write the three or four main sentences of their response and to record the rest of their thoughts in a short series of notes or an outline. Let the conversation continue. Stop it again after two or three speakers, and again ask the students to respond as they did the first time. After several repetitions, ask volunteers to read what they have written.

14   HOW TO ARGUE

Whenever a debate gets emotional and listening stops, have the next speaker, before making a statement, repeat (to the satisfaction of the first speaker) what the first speaker said.

15   SELF-INVENTORY QUESTIONNAIRE

First have students fill out the following questionnaire privately; later discuss it as a group.

1. When one remains silent in the group . . .
2. In a new group, I usually . . .
3. I feel good about myself in a group when I . . .
4. I sense trust from a group when they . . .
5. People usually respond to me in a group with (by) . . .
6. I am threatened in a group when . . .
7. I feel uncomfortable in a group when the group is . . .
8. Select one: My answers reflect (a) the way I see myself, (b) the way others see me, or (c) the way I would like to be.

The questionnaire will help students think about themselves and how they respond to others and to their own feelings when they are relating to people in a group situation (such as during the debates we discussed in Strategies 13 and 14). Answering these questions and sharing some thoughts about them with the group should help students discover that we all have in common many basic human reactions, emotions, and feelings, particularly in the group situation.

16 PROGRESSIVE RELAXATION

I use this technique with my basketball team on game day. Periodically, I use it in the classroom; it is especially useful before or after finals. The technique is also useful in falling asleep.

Have students take off their shoes and lie flat on their backs on the carpet in a darkened room. Explain that they need not participate but that once you begin the exercise, they must not change the environment by laughing, coughing, or moving around. (Emphasize this point to the group repeatedly as you are getting started.) Tell them to place their hands at their sides, uncross their legs, close their eyes, and remain in this position for the entire exercise. Have students take three large breaths, let them out easily, and try to relax. When they have relaxed, have them make a fist with the right hand. Tell them to squeeze, squeeze, squeeze, then relax ... very quietly. Repeat the same process with the left fist, the right forearm, the left forearm, the whole right arm, the whole left arm. Ask them to tighten and relax, in order, the ankles, the calves, the thighs, the stomach, the neck, then both fists and both arms, then stomach and neck. Then ask them to tense the whole body and then relax—totally.

After each segment students must relax ten to fifteen seconds. Continue to speak softly, reminding them to relax. You merely work up the body part by part, then increase the number of parts that are flexing at one time. The final full tense should be all-out. The final relaxation should be as intense as the tensing. Go through the same parts of the body telling students to relax each in turn. Then, to complete relaxation of the entire body finish with directions such as these:

Feel yourself become very light.
No longer feel the floor.
Feel yourself float out of this room and into a sunny forest.
See a cabin in the forest.
Walk to the cabin very slowly. Go inside and lie down on the bed.
  Relax.

See yourself get off the bed and leave the cabin. See yourself walk away from the cabin. Slowly the picture fades all yellow. All orange. All red. All purple.
Be aware that you are back in the classroom.
With your eyes closed, sit up.
Now slowly open your eyes.

At this point, pair up the students and have one partner start tapping the other at the top of the head and down the sides, waking that person's body up, then tap back to the top. Have the students switch roles and repeat.

When the process is completed, debrief, discussing the exercise as a group. Were the students able to relax? What inhibits relaxation? Were the students able to let their imaginations flow? What did they find inhibiting their imaginations?

The entire process—relaxation and reawakening—should take about thirty-five minutes. The more often you guide it, the better your timing of the directions will become.

17   ICEBREAKER

Tell the group you need a volunteer for a little demonstration. Don't explain what the demonstration is, and don't ask for volunteers. Merely ask the students to think about whether or not they'll volunteer.

After one minute, ask one student if he or she carried on an internal conversation during the pause. How did the conversation go, and why? Call on other people to report their internal conversations.

Debrief. Ask the students: Do you trust the teacher? How is trust built? Should you automatically trust people? What inhibits trust? Were you afraid of what others might think?

18   LAUGHING CHAIN

Have the class lie on the floor so that each person's head is on another's stomach. Tell the person at the top of the chain to begin laughing. Watch the laugh spread.

19   TRUST LIFTING

Ask the group: "Is there someone who is feeling particularly alienated today?" This volunteer then selects six other people from the group to participate in the strategy. Ask the student who first volunteered to lie down flat on the ground, surrounded by the chosen group. Ask the group to pick up the student, then hold him or her up as high as possible while the student remains rigid. They will then slowly and gently lower the student to the floor. Slowly, one at a time, they will remove their hands. Finally, the seven people will discuss the experience.

Ask the students: Why were the six particular people chosen? How did each student involved feel before, during, and after the exercise? What did the people on the outside observe?

20   BREAKING INTO THE GROUP

This strategy is similar in its purpose to Strategy 19. Again, ask the group: "Is there someone who is feeling alienated today who would like to volunteer for an exercise?" Class members form a circle, facing in, holding hands. The chosen student walks around the outside until he or she selects a place to break in. The student then fights to get into the circle, forcing apart the arms of the students at the chosen point of entry, and assumes a position in the circle joining hands. Sit down and discuss.

Debrief. Why did the student feel alienated in the first place? Of what significance was the spot where the student tried to break the circle and enter? How did the people at the point of breaking in respond? Did they resist? Did they give in too easily?

21   NAME TAGS

Members of the class make name tags, but instead of writing only their names on the tags, students use adjectives that describe themselves. After pinning on the name tags, students mill around reading each other's tags.

Next, people turn their tags over and list factual information such as name, address, age, phone, and so on. Again, they mill around and read each other's tags.

Finally, people decide which side of the tag they prefer to expose. Students may explain individual decisions or participate in a general discussion.

22 DYADS

Have students go off in pairs to different parts of the room to get acquainted with each other. One student asks questions for three minutes; then the other student has three minutes to ask questions. At the end of six minutes, students come back to the big circle and introduce their partners to the entire group.

23 BLIND WALK

Students pair up; one student in each pair is blindfolded. The seeing partners grasp the hands of the blinded partners and lead them around outside. The seeing partners ask the blindfolded partners to touch certain things while on the walk. The seeing partners are entirely responsible for giving directions that allow the blindfolded partners to negotiate the walk. Have the students reverse roles and repeat the strategy. Back in the classroom, the group discusses the exercise.

Debrief. Ask your students the following questions: When you were walking blind, did you receive good directions? Did you trust your partner? How did your partner inhibit or enhance your trust? What pleasant experiences did you have? Did you feel trust in the way your blindfolded partner held onto you?

24 I TRUST YOU TO CATCH ME

Have students pair off. Ask one student to stand an arm's length from the other, back turned to the partner. The person behind holds arms straight out; the person in front falls straight back into the arms of the catcher. Have the partners reverse roles.

Have each pair of partners discuss their experience, then discuss as a group.

25   I TRUST YOU TO PASS ME

Have all the students line up in one line facing the same direction, alternating boy and girl. The two largest students should be first and second in line; they become "helpers." All the students in the line put their arms up over their heads. While remaining rigid, the helpers then pick up the third person in line. That person is slowly, carefully passed down the line (face up) over the heads of the students. Even the school's largest students can be passed in this manner.

Once everyone has been passed, discuss the experience as a group.

26   MIND TEASER

Have students take the test given below.[2] Read the questions to the students, allowing only about twenty seconds for each answer. Discuss the students' answers and the hidden assumptions in each question.

1. When a cone is bisected by a horizontal, the remaining base segment is called a "frustum." What is the remaining uppermost segment called?

2. Give the first names of the following famous people: Dante, Rembrandt, Michelangelo.

3. Two men played chess. They played five games. Each man won three games. How?

4. How far can a dog run into the woods?

5. Mike Smith is a New York resident with a Georgia mother, but his father is Norwegian. Mike is not yet 21. Why can't he be buried in Georgia?

6. What is the common link that unites a guinea pig's tail, a shark's sleeping habit, and a rat's incidence of nausea.

7. Even if he and his family are on the verge of starvation, an Eskimo male will not attempt to eat a penguin's egg. Why?

---

[2]Excerpts from "The What-Me-Stupid? Quiz" by Jack Sharkey. Originally appeared in *Playboy* Magazine; copyright © 1977 by Playboy.

8. An archaeologist reported that in the desert near Jerusalem he had discovered two gold coins dated 439 B.C. Do you believe him?

9. If you had one match and you entered a room to start a kerosene lamp, an oil heater, and a wood-burning stove, which would you light first, and why?

10. What does a ship weigh when leaving port?

11. Arrange four nines (9, 9, 9, 9) in a formula (divide, multiply, add, subtract, and so forth) so that they total 100. Each nine can be used only once.

12. You have found a dime in an empty wine bottle. The bottle is corked. Your job is to get the dime out of the bottle without taking the cork out. You must not damage the bottle in any way. How do you remove the dime?

13. Explain this true boast: In my bedroom, the nearest lamp that I usually keep turned on is twelve feet away from my bed. Alone in the room, without using wires, string, or any other aids or contraptions, I can turn out that lamp and get into bed before the room is dark.

14. What is the main characteristic of a Hawaiian snake? an Icelandic snake? an Irish snake?

15. Supply the next item in each of the following series:
77   49   36   18   _____
O   T   T   F   F   S   S   _____
April 5   May 3   _____

16. Which of the following sentences does not contain a grammatical error?
Susie loves Billy more than me.
Susie loves Billy more than I.

17. In the following list of reindeer names, write down the ones that do *not* pull Santa's sleigh through the sky on Christmas Eve: Dasher, Dancer, Prancer, Vixen, Comet, Cupid, Donner, Blitzen, Rudolph, Dixon, and Watson.

18. On a piece of paper draw nine dots in a three-by-three pattern (as shown), and then draw four straight lines through all nine dots without lifting pen or pencil from the paper.

```
• • •
• • •
• • •
```

Answers:

1. A cone.

2. These *are* their first names.

3. They didn't play each other.

4. Halfway. After that, he's going out.

5. He is alive.

6. Nothing links them, because none of them exist.

7. Penguins don't lay eggs.

8. "B.C." couldn't be used until *after* Christ was born.

9. The match.

10. Its anchor.

11. $99 + (9 \div 9)$, or $99 + \frac{9}{9}$.

12. Push the cork into the bottle, and shake the dime out.

13. It's daytime.

14. None of these places has snakes.

15. (a) 8; because 7 times 7 is 49, 4 times 9 is 36, and so on. (b) E. The letters are the initials of one, two, three, four, and so on. (c) June 4; June, with four letters, is the next logical month in the series of months. April has five letters; May has three.

16. Both are correct. The first means "Susie loves Billy more than she loves me"; the second means "Susie loves Billy more than I love Billy."

17. If you didn't mark out all the names, don't you think you are a little old to continue believing in Santa Claus?

18.

27 PAPER AIRPLANE CONTEST

Jeffrey Shrank, in his book *Teaching Human Beings,* asks the questions, "Why do most classrooms have high ceilings?" In September, I wrote this question on the board and told the students when they had the answer, they would get a surprise. The answer? "So that paper airplanes can fly."

By October they'd figured it out, and we had a paper-airplane contest, after looking into some of the wonderful books that tell how to build the planes. The beginning math class members served as judges. We gave prizes for the longest flight (in distance), the longest time in the air, the best and most creative designs, and a booby prize.

28 FRICTION DAY

After a class session in which friction has taken place between you and the class, at the next class meeting, invite the class outside into the warm sunshine. Just sit quietly. Every so often, a student may come up to you and talk for a while. By the following class period, the atmosphere will be back to normal.

4 Group Concept at Work

29   SCORE AS MUCH AS POSSIBLE

This strategy by Jeffery Shrank will graphically illustrate the concept of cooperation/competition.

> The simulation game described here[3] is one in which success will be proportionate to the ability of the group to cooperate with each other rather than to compete. Because our culture values competition and teaches it in school most people when put in a game situation (or any situation) will try to "beat" the other guy (or defend themselves). This game makes that hidden assumption clear and raises questions about its value.
>
> The game works with groups of eight. After ten rounds of "Score as Much as Possible," the final scores are totaled for the group or groups and invariably the group will have fallen together, having failed to "score as much as possible." Group members are not told that they are to compete with each other, nor are they told to cooperate; they are left to assume which is correct. Rarely is the assumption even questioned; competition is quickly assumed to be the proper stance.
>
> After the game, analyze why the competition assumption was made and how it influenced the final score. Discuss how this assumption affects our society in both entertainment and business. Envision how a society would be different if people made a cooperation assumption instead of a competition assumption. Discuss a grading system for a class that would give the entire class the lowest grade scored by any one of its members. Invent a game which would still be fun but would be based on cooperation instead of competition.
>
> *Rules for "Score as Much as Possible"*
>
> For the game the group should be divided into groups of eight and positioned in movable desks, chairs, or seated on the floor like this:

[3]Reprinted from *Teaching Human Beings: 101 Subversive Activities for the Classroom.* Copyright © 1972 by Jeffrey Shrank. Reprinted by permission of Beacon Press.

There can be many groups of eight in one room if necessary. Each group operates independently of the others: there is no competition or cooperation between groups. Within each group are four sets of partners. If the group is not divisible exactly by eight, some can act as judges, score-keepers, and time-keepers. After the people are grouped, give out the score sheet for the game, one to each set of partners (four to a group). Tell them to study the score sheet for about four minutes and try to figure out how to play the game. Be sure to mention the title of the game out loud.

After the four minutes, tell the groups the following rules:
1. You may confer only with your partner unless otherwise instructed (as they will be in rounds 5, 8, and 10). Secret signals are not allowed.
2. Each set of partners must agree on a single choice for each round— an X or a Y.

Begin playing the game. Each set of partners should fill in the score sheet as the game progresses. Sample scoring for a round: Let's say that in one group one set of partners chooses X and the other three choose Y. According to the score sheet, the partners that chose the X would win three points while the three sets of partners who chose Y would each lose one point. Note that on rounds 5, 8, and 10, group consultation is allowed and the scores are doubled, tripled, or quintupled. Conduct each round; keep time; inform the groups when they can consult and when choices must be made; make sure everyone is following the rules.

After round 10, each group of eight should figure out its total score. Here is the catch. The title of the game, "Score as Much as Possible" refers to the group as a whole and not to the partners. The idea of the game is for the group to score as many points as possible. If they all chose Y for each round, the group total would be plus 100. The group's success is judged by how close they came to a perfect game of plus 100. Many, if not most, groups will have scores below zero because of the assumption that competition was in order rather than cooperation.

After the final scoring, discuss what hidden assumptions the players made, why that assumption was made, how it hurt the total score, and in what other areas of life those same assumptions are made. Discuss any relationship between the game and the test given earlier. Discuss the group process during the game.

Score Sheet for "Score as Much as Possible"

Directions: For ten rounds you and your partner will choose either an X or a Y. The points scored in each round are dependent upon the pattern of choice made by everyone in the group. Scoring will be according to the following:

4 Xs	Lose 1 point each
3 Xs	Win 1 point each
1 Y	Lose 3 points
2 Xs	Win 2 points each
2 Ys	Lose 2 points each
1 X	Win 3 points
3 Ys	Lose 1 point each
4 Ys	Win 1 point each

Strategy: You can confer with your partner once each round and make a joint decision. Before rounds 5, 8, and 10 you can confer with the other members of the group.

Round	Time	Confer with	Choice	Points won	Points lost	
1	1 min.	partner				
2	30 sec.	partner				
3	30 sec.	partner				
4	30 sec.	partner				
5	2 min. 30 sec.	group partner				Bonus round double score
6	30 sec.	partner				
7	30 sec.	partner				
8	3 min. 30 sec.	group partner				Bonus round triple score
9	30 sec.	partner				
10	3 min. 30 sec.	group partner				Bonus round Multiply score by 5.
						TOTAL

30   HUMAN MACHINE

One person gets up in the front of the room and makes one small mechanical movement; one by one people get up and, reacting to the action or creating a new one, attach themselves to a growing "machine." Soon all are acting as parts of one large mechanical system. Get the machine going and keep it going for a few minutes.

Debrief. What kept the machine working? What made it break down? Who cooperated? Who didn't? Who were the designers? Who were the workers?

Do the same exercise in groups of five or six.

Debrief. Is it easier to achieve cooperation in small groups or large? To what social groups might this "people as machine" analogy apply? Think about clubs, states, ethnic groups, or nations.

31   GROUP BUILDING WITH HANDS

Divide the class into groups of five or six. Have them get on their knees and build whatever item you assign them to build (you might suggest a house, a car, an animal, or the like) using only their hands as materials.

Then let them build items of their own choosing, again using no other materials but their hands.

Debrief. Who cooperated? Who designed? Who destroyed? Upon what is cooperation based?

32   SILENT GROUP BUILDING

Divide the class into groups of five or six. Ask each group to build, *without talking,* a structure out of newspaper. Gestures and sign language may be used, but group members may not talk to one another. At the end of ten minutes, judge each structure in relation to the other structures with regard to height and stability.

After the judging, have each group determine what role each member played in the building process. Were they workers, helpers, designers, foremen, or goof-offs?

Form new groups with all those who played the same role forming a group. Repeat the exercise. Did the structures improve or get worse? Was more cooperation apparent, or less? What contributes to or hinders building a successful working group?

33   TEACHING AND LEARNING NEW ACTIVITIES

Ask each student to list five activities (horseback riding, building, swimming, fishing, or the like) he or she most enjoys doing and feels confident to teach to someone else.

Then ask each student to list five things he or she would like to do or learn to do.

Match people up on the basis of the lists, and ask students to arrange to meet their partners over the weekend both to teach and to learn one activity. On Monday, discuss the experiences of the weekend. Many new friendships, interests, and discoveries will result.

34 DECISIONS: LOST ON THE MOON

This strategy has been shared by thousands of groups; I don't know its original source. Pass out a sheet with the following directions on it:

You are in a space crew originally scheduled to rendezvous with a mother ship on the lighted surface of the moon. Mechanical difficulties, however, have forced your ship to crash land on the dark side of the moon at a spot some 200 miles from the rendezvous point. The rough landing damaged much of the equipment aboard. Since survival depends on reaching the mother ship, only the most critical of the remaining items must be chosen for the 200-mile trip. Below are listed fifteen items left intact after landing. Your task is to rank them in order of their importance to your crew as it attempts to reach the rendezvous point. Place the number 1 by the most important item, and so on, through number 15, which indicates the least important item.

_____ box of matches

_____ food concentrates

_____ 50-foot nylon rope

_____ parachute silk

_____ portable heating unit

_____ two 45-caliber pistols

_____ one case dehydrated milk

_____ solar-powered FM receiver transmitter

_____ two 100-pound tanks of oxygen

_____ stellar map of the moon's constellations

_____ life raft

_____ magnetic compass

_____ five gallons of water

_____ signal flares

_____ first-aid kit, with injec-
tion needles

Discuss the students' choices and why they were made.

35 DECISIONS: LOST IN THE CITY

Give each of your students ten cents, two bus tokens, and a map of the city. Blindfold them, and drop them off all over the city in obscure places. They are to return to a central location, having plotted the most direct route on the city map. The first student to arrive at the central location wins.

You might have your local sheriff's Search and Rescue Unit develop a similar strategy for outdoor terrain. Variables might include the weather, the terrain, use of food and water, reading a compass and map. Steven Daniel's book *How 2 Gerbils* . . . suggests a similar exercise.

36 PROBLEM-SOLVING AND DECISION-MAKING PROCESSES

Discuss the following methods:

General Method
1. Define the problem.
2. List alternative solutions.
3. List costs/benefits of each alternative.
4. List possible negative and positive results of each alternative.
5. Decide upon a course of action.
6. After the decision is enacted, determine its true effects.
7. Reevaluate the situation
8. Learn to live with decisions.

St. Ignatius Method
1. Determine choices.
2. List, in priority, the advantages or disadvantages of each choice.
3. Give each advantage a positive numerical value and each disadvantage a negative numerical value.
4. Add up the values of each choice.
5. Make decision based on total of numerical value.

Personal Decisions
1. Ask yourself: What is the worst possible result? Is it worth the risk?
2. Remember: You must be responsible for your own decisions and their consequences.
3. *No decision* is in fact a decision—it is the decision not to decide and thus to maintain the status quo.
4. Ask yourself: Am I functioning on a logical or emotional level?
5. How do the other people involved view the problem? How will they view my decision?
6. Who around me will lend support? Who will lead in blocking me? Why?
7. How will I use the support? How will I overcome the blockage?

Researching
1. What do I need to know to make a decision?
2. How can I find out?
3. What will be valid research?
4. Study fallacious thinking and statements and avoid them in your own research.

Scientific Method
1. Observe.
2. Develop a hypothesis.
3. Test the hypothesis.
4. Make a statement of the truth or knowledge gained.
5. Retest on the basis of new information.

Brainstorming Techniques
1. List on the blackboard as fast as possible as many alternative solutions as you can think of.
2. Go back and develop priorities among the alternatives.
3. Make a decision.

37   APPLIED PROBLEM SOLVING

Ask students to choose a problem or decision and resolve it by making use of one of the processes described in Strategy 36. They should then write papers explaining the process used and justifying the resolution. Have the students exchange papers and write critiques of one another's papers.

38   EMPLOYING A TECHNIQUE

Present the class with a problem, and divide the students into groups of five or six. Assign one problem-solving technique to each group, and ask each group to work on the problem from the perspective of its assigned technique.

  Debrief. Each group must determine the background of the problem, define the problem, state the alternatives, note where blockage will result, note what the results of each course of action might be, and finally recommend a solution. The goal of each group is to prepare an integrated paper, developed through the group process, explaining how its particular technique was applied to resolving the problem.

39   SOLVE THE CRIME FROM THE CLUES

This strategy was given to me by an English instructor at Arizona State University. You'll need to type out the following clues and give one clue to each member of the class:

  When he was discovered dead, Mr. Kelley had a bullet hole in his thigh and a knife wound in his back.

  Mr. Jones shot at an intruder in his apartment building at 12 midnight.

  The elevator operator reported to police that he had seen Mr. Kelley at 12:15 A.M.

  The bullet taken from Mr. Kelley's thigh matched those used in the gun owned by Mr. Jones.

  Only one bullet had been fired from Mr. Jones's gun.

When the elevator man saw Mr. Kelley, Mr. Kelley was bleeding slightly, but he did not seem too badly hurt.

A knife with Mr. Kelley's blood on it was found in Miss Smith's yard.

The knife found in Miss Smith's yard had Mr. Scott's fingerprints on it.

Mr. Kelley had destroyed Mr. Jones's business by stealing his customers.

The elevator man saw Mr. Kelley's wife go to Mr. Scott's apartment at 11:30 P.M.

The elevator operator said that Mr. Kelley's wife frequently left the building with Scott.

Mr. Kelley's body was found in the park.

Mr. Kelley's body was found at 1:30 A.M.

Mr. Kelley had been dead for one hour when his body was found, according to a medical report.

The elevator man saw Mr. Kelley go to Mr. Scott's room at 12:25 A.M.

It was obvious from the condition of Mr. Kelley's body that it had been dragged a long distance.

Miss Smith saw Mr. Kelley go to Mr. Jones's apartment at 11:55 P.M.

Mr. Kelley's wife disappeared after the murder.

Police were unable to locate Mr. Scott after the murder. When police tried to locate Mr. Jones after the murder, they discovered that he had disappeared.

The elevator man said that Miss Smith was in the lobby of the apartment building when he went off duty.

Miss Smith often followed Mr. Kelley.

Mr. Jones had told Mr. Kelley that he was going to kill him.

Mr. Kelley's bloodstains were found in Mr. Scott's car.

Mr. Kelley's bloodstains were found on the carpet in the hall outside Mr. Jones's apartment.

Miss Smith said that nobody left the apartment building between 12:25 A.M. and 12:45 A.M.

Some class members may end up with more than one clue. Tell them they have all the information necessary to solve the crime. Tell them they have thirty-five minutes to tell you who got murdered, who the murderer was, and the time, place, motive, and weapon. Do not tell them whether they are correct until they have made all decisions. Do not indicate which guesses are wrong and which correct; just indicate that their answers are wrong—this eliminates mere guessing on each item.

Answer: After receiving a superficial gunshot wound, from Mr. Jones, Mr. Kelley went to Mr. Scott's apartment where he was killed by Mr. Scott with a knife at 12:30 A.M., because Mr. Scott was in love with Mr. Kelley's wife.

Discuss the process used to solve the case. What method worked? What methods didn't? What method would be the most efficient? Who helped? Who didn't? Why? Why not?

40 WHO GETS THE MONEY?

Select eight volunteers who want to win $1.75 while risking only $ .25 Have them sit in a circle with the rest of the class seated in a larger, outside circle. Place the quarters in a pile in the center of the small circle. Tell the volunteers they must decide which of them will get the money—but all must agree to the distribution method within a specified amount of time.

As they suggest alternatives, ask them if they all agree to the method. Once they have decided, make sure the agreed-upon person gets the money. If they make no decision in the time allowed, the money will be turned over to the Student Council General Fund or to some other unit from which the class will receive no direct benefit.

Have the volunteers discuss how they made their decision, and why. Did their greed surface in the discussion as it had when they volunteered for the exercise?

Then allow the observers, who remained silent during the strategy, to offer their observations.

41 THE WORLD DOUBLED LAST NIGHT

This strategy by Jeffrey Shrank addresses decision making about relative terms, objects, events:

Tell the students that last night while they were all asleep the entire universe doubled in size. Try to have them prove that it did not. Of course, all the scales and rulers also doubled in size, so measuring will be no good. The real question is that if everything changes in the same degree and in the same relation as everything else is there really any change at all?[4]

Discuss other judgments we make that are highly relative: true beauty, good personality, quite intelligent, rather strong, and so on.

42 NO ONE LISTENS

Give the students a problem to be solved. Divide the class into groups of four or five. Have all the people in the groups talk at once about the problem and its solutions. No one is to listen to anyone else.

Debrief. What were the frustrations? What is the difference between *hearing* and *listening*? Do parents *listen* to or *hear* their children? Do teachers *hear* students or students *hear* teachers?

43 HOW DO YOU REACT TO PROBLEMS?

Ask the students to write down how they most normally react to a serious problem. Do they *think* first? *act* first? *feel* first?

Debrief. Discuss the answers of each member of the group. Why do they react as they do? Which reaction is most appropriate? Which reaction is normal? Do boys react in the same way as girls? adults the same as teenagers? Is there a logical sequence of reactions?

44 THE ROLES WE PLAY IN DISCUSSION

Give ten members of the class role descriptions—which they are to keep to themselves. Give the students who have not been given roles a list of all the roles you assigned. Then give the role players a problem to solve—a realistic, current problem that affects the students. Have

[4]Reprinted from *Teaching Human Beings: 101 Subversive Activities for the Classroom.* Copyright © 1972 by Jeffrey Shrank. Reprinted by permission of Beacon Press.

the role players discuss the problem for five to ten minutes. Stop the discussion and ask the rest of the students to guess who was playing what role. Discuss how and why they arrived at their answers.

Chairperson: You see yourself as a coordinator of the group; you see yourself as the leader, and you enjoy the role.

Casper Milktoast: You have good ideas but never say anything unless asked; you are too shy to put yourself in the limelight.

Dictator: You feel you could do a much better job of being chairman, and you set out to become chairperson.

Wishy-Washy: You go from problem to problem, question to question, solution to solution; you are sincere but unorganized.

Agreer: You cut in before people have finished their sentence, because you know what they are going to say. You restate and reclarify everyone's statements.

Socrates: You are continually asking deep philosophical questions rather than dealing with the realities of the problem.

Fifth Column: You see this whole process as nonsense and spend your time giving your ideas in a low voice to your neighbors.

Pollyanna: You try to agree with all points of view and make sure no one gets upset or feels bad about how the group treats their ideas.

Jester: You are the group clown; you try to take each opportunity to make a joke.

Boy Scout: You are warm, friendly, thrifty, prepared, and so on, and attempt to get the problem solved as if you were on a time schedule.

After this strategy students should take this list to a city council or school board meeting and identify those who play the same roles. Discuss the meeting in class.

45   GROUP PROBLEM SOLVING

Divide the class into groups of five to seven. Give each group a short paragraph describing a different, multi-faceted problem such as:

You and your spouse are traveling across the country. Your car breaks down in the middle of the hot Nevada desert. You have seen no traffic on the road. There is a town about five miles to the west (you have been traveling south). You have no cash and you are not sure the small-town merchants will accept credit cards. Your spouse is afraid to stay in the car alone, and you are afraid to leave the car, as you can't lock it. You are also uncertain whether you and/or your spouse could walk the five miles in the tremendous heat. What are the range of problems that face you? What alternatives are available to you? What do you decide?

Ask each group to solve its problem by making a choice of a plan of action. A group recorder keeps notes on the *process* and on why the choice was made.

All the groups come together. Each problem is read and each group justifies its decision. The other groups offer critiques on *process* and *techniques.*

46   ROLE PLAYING PERSONAL PROBLEMS

Ask each student to describe, on a five-by-eight-inch card, a current personal problem. (The situation should be described in such a way that the student can remain anonymous.) The cards are collected and shuffled. A volunteer chooses a card, then selects the number of people needed to act out the problem and its solution. Role play all of the situations given in the cards.

Debrief. How realistic were the role playings? Could the students identify with the actors? Were their solutions realistic? Did they get emotionally involved in the problems?

47   MAKING PERSONAL DECISIONS

Read the statements listed below, or a similar group of statements applicable to your school or locale, one at a time. After the first statement in each group is read, ask the students to line up against the chalkboard at a point in the line that expresses their agreement or disagreement with the value implied in the statement. A position to the far right expresses total agreement, one to the far left expresses total disagreement, and the exact center position indicates indecision. Then read the next statement in the group, and ask the students if they would like to move according to their feelings.

1. A. An eighteen-year-old high school student smokes marijuana at home while his parents are gone.
   B. A father of three smokes dope while his children are away for the weekend.
2. A. A high school boy tells his girl friend he'll marry her if she'll have sex with him first.
   B. A high school girl tells her boy friend she'll marry him if he'll have sex with her first.
3. A. A beautiful girl becomes a prostitute in order to build up her savings account.
   B. A beautiful girl becomes a prostitute in order to feed her baby; she can find no other job.
4. A. The school has denied students the right to read books written by communists.
   B. The school has denied students the right to read pornographic books.
   C. The school has denied your student council the right to an opening prayer at its meetings.
   D. Students shout down a John Birch Society speaker on campus.

After all statements in the group have been read, and the students have moved accordingly, ask the class to sit down.[5]
Debrief the decision-making process.

[5] Adapted from *Values Clarification: A Handbook of Strategies for Teachers and Students* by Sidney B. Simon, Leland W. Howe, and Howard Kirschenbaum, copyright 1972 Hart Publishing Company, Inc.

Social Psychology

Section 1, Social Myths and Values, introduces students to the areas of concern of social psychology.

The strategies in Section 2, Perceptions: Senses and the Self, first isolate each sense, heighten its awareness, and then stimulate it. A group of strategies then follow that are designed to stimulate all the senses simultaneously so that the students will become more aware of their surroundings. The class will have a great deal of fun with these strategies; they are a nonthreatening means of further developing the group concept.

At the beginning of the term, students may be somewhat reluctant to begin verbal exchange immediately. The goal of the strategies in Section 3, Verbal and Nonverbal Communication, is to break down this initial doubt through positive feedback.

The next five sections are arranged in a developmental order to reflect the individual's process of becoming acquainted with his or her environment. Strategies concerned with child development, personality, love/marriage, death, and loneliness give students a clearer picture of the place they occupy in the scheme of life. Through simulation, role playing, and discussion, students take a look at themselves and their place in the modern technological world and develop an awareness of how others see them.

These strategies, while emphasizing skills such as oral interaction, development of perceptions, introspection, and values clarification are geared more toward the study of particular subject matter than were the strategies in Unit I. For these exercises to be effective, however, it is strongly recommended that you first build a sense of group through the use of the strategies in the first unit.

1 Social Myths and Values

To introduce the domain of social psychology, give students the Social Inquiry Introductory Test and discuss their answers.

Answer true or false to all questions.

1. A low forehead means a low level of intelligence.
2. People probably never learn anything while they are deeply asleep.
3. A fine line separates genius and insanity.
4. Frequent masturbation leads to feeblemindedness.
5. A person who learns quickly remembers longer than a person who learns more slowly.
6. All people in America are born with equal capacity for achievement.
7. Animals lower than man are able to reason.
8. Famous men tend to be born of poor but hard-working parents.
9. The intelligence of the average Indian is inferior to that of the dullest white person.
10. Lessons learned just before going to sleep are remembered better than those learned early in the morning.
11. If a child must be punished, it is best to let the father do it.
12. Infants learn nothing until they are about a year old.
13. A law of compensation exists in nature; blind people are born with a highly developed sense of touch.
14. An especially favorable environment can probably raise the IQ a few points.

Answers

1. (F) No one has been able to prove a correspondence between physical characteristics and intelligence.

2. (T) Some learning occurs prior to actually going to sleep, but nothing is learned while you are asleep.

3. (F) This notion is popular primarily because the general population doesn't relate very well to either extreme.

4. (F) Masturbation causes no physical damage: telling children such stories can lead to their having psychological problems due to guilt.

5. (F) How long it took to learn something has nothing to do with how well or long you retain it; learning is learning.

6. (F) Everyone is born with varying capabilities. People handicapped either physically or mentally may have some severe limitations. The environment can lead to changes in abilities after birth as well.

7. (T) Some of the animals that are thought to reason include the chimpanzee, the porpoise, and the ant.

8. (F) This concept is popular in American mythology, but for every Lincoln and log cabin, there is a Franklin Delano Roosevelt with millionaire parents.

9. (F) Not only is intelligence extremely difficult to measure (and most tests that attempt to do so are culturally biased), but no one has been able to substantiate intelligence differences among races. While an Eskimo might not do too well with Einstein's computers, Einstein probably wouldn't have lasted long by himself in the Arctic either.

10. (T) The last things you learn at night tend to stay with you longer, because no new learning situations develop while you sleep that might interfere with recall.

11. (F) For both parents to share equally in the disciplining is best.

12. (F) Special cameras show that infants are learning about their environment and making adjustments while in the womb.

13. (F) This popular belief is untrue; people with handicaps in one area tend to learn acute use of senses in other areas in order to function as normally as possible—but their abilities are learned, not inborn.

14. (T) An environment that provides warmth, security, and intellectual stimulation is much more likely to affect IQ positively than a negative environment.

49   VALUES CLARIFICATION

Choose a topic that is currently being discussed, such as war, racism, abortion, or a similar controversial topic. Have students brainstorm a list of statements concerning the topic.

Students will then list these statements on a piece of paper. Following each statement, students will place either SA (strongly agree), A (agree), D (disagree), or SD (strongly disagree).

To make use of the lists, you may exercise a number of options. The suggested strategies will place students into situations where they must clarify their values and will allow them the opportunity to discuss those values and attempt to influence the thinking of others with regard to them.

Option 1: Group all those who responded the same way to a statement. After discussion, a spokesperson from each group will explain some of the reasons the group members feel as they do.

Option 2: Have the students line up according to how strongly they feel about a statement. Those at the far left would be willing to die to uphold the statement; those at the far right would be willing to die to oppose it. Allow three minutes for people to lobby those on each side of them in an attempt to get them to change their positions. At the end of the three minutes, stop the conversations and allow people to change places.

Option 3: Have students merely state their positions on the statement and field questions from those who disagree with their views.

For other values-clarification strategies, see the exercises found in Sidney Simon's, Leland Howe's, and Howard Kirschenbaum's *Values Clarification.* See also Sidney Simon's and Jay Clark's *Beginning Values Clarification.* The broad-based exercises in these two books can, with a little creative thought, be adapted to almost any subject.

2 Perceptions: Senses and the Self

50 TALKING HANDS

Ask students to stand in a circle, close their eyes, and begin to mill around, quietly bumping into each other. After one minute, ask the students to stop—still without making any noise. It is most important that no noise be made throughout this entire strategy—it would give away who and where certain students are in the room.

Pair up students as they continue to keep their eyes closed and remain quiet. As you pair them up, have the partners face one another and grab hands. Students at this age feel more comfortable during this strategy when they are matched up boy–girl. Again, students must remain quiet, with eyes closed.

Explain to the students that they are now going to carry on a conversation, using only their hands to do the talking. They are to keep their hands grasped the entire time with their eyes closed and without making any noise.

Tell the students to say hello to their partners. Ask them to tell their partners that they feel great. Ask one partner to express to the other that he or she is having a bad day, and ask the partner to respond, in hand talk, by saying, "I hope you have a better day." Finally, ask them to tell their partners that they have enjoyed talking to them and wish them goodbye, with eyes still closed. Direct them to drop hands and to open their eyes. An immediate laugh usually results.

Debrief. Discuss the exercise with the group. Did they understand the messages their partners gave with their hands? Did they think they had identified their partners? Were they correct? Did they enjoy this strategy?

51 TERRITORIAL INTERVIEW

Have a student volunteer to leave the room until called to return to participate in a very nonthreatening exercise. After the student leaves, explain the concept of territoriality (the space around yourself that you stake out and don't like anyone to enter). Ask someone in the group to volunteer to "interview" the returning student about some subject that student would find easy to discuss. At first, the interviewer is to stand about twenty feet from the interviewee, then move slowly closer and closer with each question. The rest of the group is to observe the interviewee's reactions to this invasion of private space and the size of the territory he or she claims. Remind the class not to laugh or react so as to suggest to the interviewee that anything unusual is occurring. The interviewer should attempt to get as close as the interviewee will allow. Discuss the event as a group.

Debrief. Did the interviewee express a sense of territoriality? What reactions did the students observe? How did the interviewee feel? the interviewer?

52   AMERICA: THE VISUAL SOCIETY

Discuss the proposition that America is a visual society rather than a listening society. Point out the importance of television as compared to radio. List words we use that reflect that we are a visual rather than audio-oriented society (the word "reflect" as used in that sentence is one example). Other examples include:

"reflects" versus "echoes"
"see the light" versus "hear the answer"
"Do you see now?" versus "Do you hear me?"
"Look for the answer." versus "Listen for the answer."
"Seeing is believing."
"I see what you mean."

Discuss why we as a society seem to be visually oriented.

53   POTATO OBSERVATION

Give each student a potato to examine closely. All the potatos are then put in the center of the circle of students and mixed up. Each student then tries to reidentify his or her own potato. Once the original potato is found, each student is to introduce his or her potato to the person to the right. Discuss the students' powers of observation.

54   WHO'S THE KILLER?

Pass out playing cards. The student who gets the ace of spades is the killer. The group can sit or mill around in a dim room. The killer "kills" by winking at another person, who waits three seconds and then falls over. The killer may be accused whenever anyone sees him or her "kill." A false accusation removes the accuser from the game.[1]

55   LOOKING INTO A LIGHT FOR COLOR

This strategy is fun—but you must convey the directions *very carefully,* especially to younger students.

Students are to look into any moderately bright light for a *split second*—only long enough to quickly open and close their eyes. If done properly, the quick glance at such a light is not dangerous. Students should avoid looking into the sun, arc lamps, or similar very bright sources.

Ask the students to close their eyes after looking into the light and concentrate on the colors they see on the eyelids. The colors can be varied according to how tightly the lids are held shut.

Debrief. Discuss with the group what they saw. Define color. Ask them to try to explain color to a blind person.

56   OBSERVING THE EYE

Have students pair up (again, the boy–girl pairing is most effective) and kneel knee-to-knee. Ask the partners to look into one another's eyes. This exercise is not a staring contest. Students are to observe how the pupil of the eye seems to have rounded edges; how a person's eyes are not *just* brown or blue but contain spots of various colors.

When you notice particularly interesting or beautiful eyes in the group, have everyone take a look.

Debrief. Discuss how students thought about eyes before this close observation. What can one tell about people from their eyes?

---

[1]Adapted from *Will the Real Teacher Please Stand Up: A Primer in Humanistic Education,* with permission of the Goodyear Publishing Company, Inc.

57   WITCH OF THE WEST

Students sit in a circle on the floor, with a broom in the center. Only one direction is given: once you understand the game, get up and play.

Pick up the broom and clear your throat very subtly. Say, "The Witch of the West is a very good witch, but the Witch of the East is better." Then say, "Yea!" and drop the broom

Have a few students, to whom you've secretly explained the game beforehand repeat the subtle throat-clearing but vary what's said and the method of dropping the broom.

Individuals "in the know" continue to take turns, varying the saying or the way they stand or drop the broom or the person at whom they look. Any member of the group who believes he or she has discovered the secret may attempt to duplicate the action. Correct attempts are "yeaed" and incorrect attempts "booed" by those who know the secret. These people keep taking turns when no volunteers offer to try. The longer the game goes on, the more obvious the throat-clearing clue should become.

58   TASTING AN ORANGE

Give an orange to each student. The students are to examine the orange in great detail. Guide their examination with directions such as these:

Feel the orange all over.
Smell the orange.
Break the skin with a thumbnail and smell the juices.
Peel the orange very slowly, smelling it as you go.
Very slowly, break the peeled orange into sections, paying particular attention to how the juices spurt.
Smell each section.
Put one small section into your mouth, but don't bite it.
Bite down slowly.
Eat the orange very slowly.
Feed a section to your neighbor.

Once the orange has been eaten, have students write down one word—other than "juicy"—that describes the taste of an orange. Discuss the exercise, focussing particular attention on the adequacy of words used to describe senses. Try the same experiment with homemade bread.

Debrief. Do we eat food and enjoy it, or do we merely consume it?

59   FOOD AND CULTURE

Read aloud the following piece on food and culture:

> To the orthodox Muslim, our use of pork is revolting, and to the orthodox
> Hindu, the thought of eating beef is almost as horrifying as the thought of
> eating human flesh is to us. To many people a crisply roasted grasshopper
> is more palatable than a raw oyster. East Africans find eggs nauseating,
> and Chinese students have sometimes become ill at seeing people drink
> milk.[2]

   Debrief. Are we what we eat? Do we eat to live or live to eat? Why
does half the world starve while the other half diets?

60   THE FAKE FIGHT

While class is in session, have the school bully and a little meek student fake a verbal argument outside the classroom. As the words get
heated, have the two students imitate the sound of one student hitting
another and a cry of pain.
   Tell the students in the classroom to write down their versions of
what happened so that you can report to the principal. After they have
handed in their accounts, tell them the incident was a big fake. Read
the paragraphs.
   Debrief. Did the students make assumptions based on what they
heard? For example, did they report automatically that a big kid had
hit the little kid? Would they be good eyewitnesses? What built-in
prejudices were revealed by the exercise?

61   SOUND IDENTIFICATION

Have everyone lie down and relax. Play a record of random sounds.
Ask the students to close their eyes and try to identify each sound they
hear by writing their guess on a piece of paper.
   Debrief. How well do we listen? Do we "listen" with our eyes as
well as our ears? How do we discriminate among the many noises that
are going on around us?

---

[2]Reprinted from *Understanding Other Cultures,* by Ina Brown, Prentice-Hall, Inc., 1963,
p. 23 by permission of the publisher.

62   SMELL BAG

Place baggies filled with spices and other "smelly" items under the noses of blindfolded students long enough for them to take one smell. Have the students write down what is in each bag. Discuss the correct answers.

Debrief. How is our sense of smell tied up with sight?

63   EXPECTATIONS AND SMELL IDENTIFICATION

A strategy suggested by Jeffrey Shrank demonstrates the role of expectations in the identification of an odor:

> An experiment using the sense of smell can be tried to demonstrate the fact that no sense is purely biological. Convince the class that you have a bottle containing a liquid known as "peppermint concentrate," an extremely powerful smell candy makers use to flavor peppermint. Place the bottle equidistant from everyone and explain that the experiment is to test who is most sensitive to smells and will detect the odor from the bottle first. A short explanation of how odors diffuse through the air with a few scientific-sounding terms such as ion rate should convince the group you are serious. The liquid should actually be water with food coloring added to convince the skeptics.
>
> Hopefully, a number of people will shortly claim they smell the faint peppermint smell. Have the group close their eyes (to concentrate better on the smell, tell them) and hold up a hand and open the eyes only when the smell is noticed. See how many bite.
>
> The demonstration is a process known as "setting." Stated simply it means that the effect of something is largely dependent on expectations. A marijuana user who sincerely believes pot causes psychotic reactions might very likely have such reactions simply because he expects them. The experiment could also serve to introduce the concept of psychosomatic illness or even prejudice.[3]

---

[3]From *Teaching Human Beings: 101 Subversive Activities for the Classroom.* Copyright © 1972 by Jeffrey Shrank. Reprinted by permission of Beacon Press.

64   SENSES FROM THE SEA

Have students rule a piece of paper into columns labeled *smell, see, hear, feel, taste*. Then ask the students to lie down and relax with blindfolds on as they listen to Rod McKuen's record, *The Sea*. Ask them to write down the words that trigger each particular sense.

Debrief. How do our senses work together and independently? How are our senses and emotions related? Discuss the lists the students have made.

65   A SENSORY TEST

Have students answer the following questions on a piece of paper. Read the questions one at a time, allowing the students about fifteen seconds to respond with a word or phrase.

1. What does red taste like?
2. What does ice cream sound like?
3. What does the smell of rain look like?
4. What does fur sound like?
5. What does soft look like?
6. How does a whisper look?
7. What does laughing taste like?

Debrief. Have the students read their answers to the class. Have them make up additional questions. Discuss the concept that the senses need each other for total fulfillment.

66   JUNK YARD TRIP

As your students learn to perceive more acutely, take them to a junk yard to find something beautiful or interesting. Put on an art show in the school, exhibiting the objects you find or construct from several objects.

Debrief. Is beauty in the eye of the beholder? Why is America a throw-away society? Is our attitude reflected in other ways besides our garbage? In what ways does the society try to change its throw-away attitude? Does the notion of body-part transplants relate to this concept? If so, how?

67 THE KOOL-AID WINO

Read aloud Richard Brautigan's story, "Kool-Aid Wino," from *Trout Fishing in America*. Explain how the two characters and Brautigan, the author, perceive a common experience as so extraordinary. Ask the students to *experience* something fully. Some students may decide to wash their hair in mayonnaise, lock themselves in dark rooms for five hours, let water drip on their foreheads for an hour, give themselves a massage with vegetable oil, open all the bottles in the cupboard and smell them, sleep at the opposite end of their beds, or go into the woods to record in writing all the sounds they hear.

The chosen experience should heighten or test a sense; this strategy is not meant to be a sociological exercise in which the activity chosen—roller skating to work or faking a jump from a building—creates an outside response. Ask students to relate their experiences to the class.

Debrief. Discuss all the concepts thus far covered concerning the senses. Which sense do we use most often? Which senses lie dormant? Ask the students to consider which sense they use most effectively; least effectively.

68 BEYOND THE SENSES

Let sense-education exercises lead you into a study of body language or altered states of consciousness—dreams, occult experiences, ESP, insanity, for example. Invite someone from your community who is involved in an occult practice to speak with the class: an astrologer, a fortune-teller, a witch, a psychic reader or healer. Ask your speaker to discuss the role of the senses in occult practice.

3 Verbal and Nonverbal Communication

69 LIMITING THE VOCABULARY

Give the following directions:

Find a quiet place and think about the words you speak. Choose four words that are important to your communication. Form groups of four, and communicate with each other for two minutes, with each person using only the four words he or she has selected.

Return to your quiet place. Cross out any words that didn't help you to communicate, and add new words to your list until you have eight words. Go back to your group and communicate for three minutes.

Repeat this process using twelve, sixteen, and twenty words, increasing the conversation time by one minute each time.

Using your list of twenty words, write a meaningful poem and read it to the class.

Debrief. Discuss how effective words are in communicating exactly what is meant. Ask if the conversations were successful attempts at communication. Determine whether words have meaning outside a particular context.

70 COMMUNICATING DIRECTIONS

Students pair up and sit back-to-back on the floor. With paper and pencil, one student in each pair draws a simple picture like the one below using squares, circles, triangles, or other simple geometric forms.

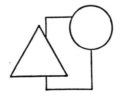

While the partners are still seated back-to-back, the artist must give the other partner directions that will allow him or her to duplicate the picture: "In the middle of the page, draw one circle one inch in diameter," and so on. Once the picture is duplicated, compare it to the original. Reverse roles.

Debrief. Discuss the difficulty of conveying exactly what one means. If it is hard to describe circles and squares, think how hard it must be to communicate about drugs, music, sex, love, or happiness.

71   MAKING POSITIVE CONTACT

Sit in the circle with the class and have a volunteer begin the strategy by looking at someone in the group and saying, "I can make positive contact with you by ... (playing football with you, smiling at you, drinking with you, whispering with you)." Everyone in the circle who wishes to verbalize should have an opportunity to do so. The person being spoken to makes no comment, nor does the rest of the group.

Debrief. Were the students surprised at the ways in which people chose to make positive contact with them? Did the choices make them feel good? surprised? unsure? How did people feel about ways that others tried to make positive contact with them?

Child Development

72 LETTER TO A BABY

Apply this strategy before beginning a unit on childbirth, and repeat it on the last day of the unit.

Ask each student to write a letter to his or her newborn baby. They might consider the following questions: What would you like to tell this child who has just come into the world? What do you know that the child should know? What is it like to live here and now? What hopes, fears, and doubts do you have for your baby?

Debrief. Have students volunteer to read their letters. Discuss.

73 HAVING CHILDREN

Watch a movie on childbirth. On the following day invite several couples into the classroom to discuss their views on and reactions to having children in their lives. For balance, you might have a couple with a large family, a couple in which the wife is a few months pregnant, adoptive parents, and a couple who are uncertain about whether they will have children or who have decided against parenthood. Let each couple present their views. Then open the discussion to questions.

You might follow this exercise with others. Invite guest speakers on rape, abortion, birth control, population growth. Arrange corresponding field trips to clinics or law-enforcement or social agencies.

74 PSYCHOLOGICAL TESTING OF SECOND GRADERS

After spending a couple of weeks on the theoretical and factual study of child development, introduce some practical experience. Arrange for your class to spend an entire day with a primary-level class so that your students can test the children and evaluate the results. The strategy works well at the second-grade level; second graders are excited about a visit from high school "big kids," they are involved in learning conceptual skills, and their verbal skills are fairly well developed. You will need to take the following steps:

1. Select a school site—preferably one of a different economic, social, and racial makeup from your own.

2. Contact the principal of the school, explain your project, and ask for suggestions regarding a second-grade teacher who might be excited about participating. Send the principal a copy of the test packet, to be shared with the interested teacher.

3. Contact the teacher and explain the project in depth. The teacher's only role is to provide space, class time, and a large name tag for each second grader.

4. Pass out copies of the previous year's packet (if you've done the strategy before), so that students can use its format as a guide to preparing their own test packet. A sample packet is included in the Appendix (page 148). The series of tests to be given to each second grader is stapled together to form one packet. Having the packet travel with each second grader is simpler than trying to assemble eight to ten single sheets per second grader at the end of the day and insures that each second grader gets to every station. The method also allows the students at each station to see the results of the other tests.

    Test in a few primary areas, using some standard techniques that have been introduced in child-development and mental health units in your class. Test motor skills, cognitive skills, affective skills. Use techniques such as open and structured interviews, free association tests, tests of physical coordination, tactile tests, ink blot tests, and others.

5. Divide your students into as many groups as you have stations. When you first arrive at the school, set up the stations—ideally in an auditorium or gymnasium. Next, have the teacher divide up the second graders arbitrarily so that each station has some students at the beginning. You'll need to do some pre-service training on how to develop rapport with second graders. Your class might even wish to spend a couple hours at a nearby school to "test your test."

6. Begin testing at 9:00 A.M. When a second grader finishes at one station, he or she should be taken by a station tester to another sta-

tion so that no child is floating from station to station. The activities at some stations will go faster than those at others; alert your students to the need to monitor the movement of the children and the pace of the day. When the second graders go to recess, get together as a group to discuss any problems with the tests and any changes that need to be made. At the noon break, eat with the teacher to discuss some of his or her pupils. The teacher is often able to offer some insights into the youngsters and may discuss in general the second-grade-level student. I've found it extremely helpful to videotape much of the day.

7. At the end of the day, you may wish to bring all the second graders together for a couple of quick exercises and to ask them about the day. What activities did they most enjoy?

8. On the following day, discuss each second grader's packet; analyze the test responses and what they indicate and what assumptions can be drawn about the second grader. Discuss the most interesting "cases" in detail. Then mail all the packets to the second-grade teacher, who often finds them beneficial in dealing with the class. Finally, discuss the techniques you've used and view the videotape.

   Don't forget to write thank you notes to the second graders and their teacher!

75   DO YOU OWN YOUR CHILDREN?

Read the class the incident reprinted below.

A mother and daughter enter a supermarket. An accident occurs when the daughter pulls the wrong orange from the pile and 37 oranges are given their freedom. The mother grabs the daughter, shakes her vigorously, and slaps her. What is your reaction? Do you ignore the incident? Do you consider it a family squabble and none of your business? Or do you go over and advise the mother not to hit her child? If the mother rejects your advice, do you physically restrain her? If she persists, do you call the police? Think about your answer for a moment.

Now let me change one detail. *The girl was not that mother's daughter.* Do you feel different? Why? Do "real" parents have the right to abuse their children because they "own" them? Now let me change another detail. Suppose the daughter was 25 years old and yelled, "Help me! Help me!" Calling the police sounded silly when I first suggested it. How does it sound with a mere change in the age of the victim? [4]

Consider the article in light of the following question: Do you own your children? Where does responsibility end and freedom begin?

---

[4]From "Parenthood Training or Mandatory Birth Control: Take Your Choice," by Roger McIntire, *Psychology Today,* October 1973. Reprinted by permission of *Psychology Today* magazine. Copyright © 1973 Ziff-Davis Publishing Company.

5 Personality

76 PERSONALITY LINEUP

Ask each student to bring to class a magazine picture illustrating his or her personality and to show the picture to no one. A quiet student may choose a picture of a slow, rambling stream on an early morning; a tomboy may choose a picture of a Raggedy Ann doll; a boy who is a musician may choose a picture of an opera house lit up at night, and so on. Attach all the girls' pictures along a wall about two feet apart and seven feet from the floor. Ask a boy to volunteer to place each girl under a picture that he feels matches her personality. Another volunteer (a girl) now places all the boys under matching pictures. Ask everyone to notice the person/picture matchups. Then ask everyone who is not under his or her own picture to sit down. Another boy volunteer re-places all the seated girls, and so on. Repeat the process until each person is under the picture he or she brought.

Debrief. On what were the matchup decisions based? Did the pictures truly match the people? Why did each person choose the picture he or she chose? What did students learn about their classmates?

77 PERSONALITY COLLAGE

Divide the class into two groups of people. Ask partners to trace one another's outlines on pieces of butcher paper that are long enough for each student to lie down on. After the students have cut out the outlines, ask them to fill out one side of the form by pasting on pictures that depict their own personalities. Partners then exchange outlines, and each partner then cuts out pictures and fills the other side of the frame with images he or she feels depict the partner's personality. Compare the two sides.[5]

---

[5]Adapted from *Will the Real Teacher Please Stand Up: A Primer in Humanistic Education*, with permission of the Goodyear Publishing Company, Inc.

Debrief. Ask the students the following questions: Do people see you as you are? as you want to be? as you think you are? What did you learn about how others see you?

78 A PICTURE OF MY PERSONALITY

Ask each student to bring in a magazine picture depicting his or her personality. With the class sitting in a circle, each student tells why the picture shows his or her personality. Some students like to include a quote with the picture.

79 YOUR NAME AND YOUR SIGNATURE

Give the following directions:

Write your name on a large piece of paper and see how it fits you. How much space does it take up on the paper? Say your name. Is it long or short? Does your name fit you? Are you too big for it? Are you too small? Or are you just right?

Imagine you had a longer name. What would it be? How do you think it would fit you? Imagine you had a shorter name. What would it be? How do you think it would fit you? Write some long names. Try them on, one at a time. See how you feel wearing them.

Write some short names. Try them on, one at a time. See how you feel wearing them. Write your own name again. Try it on again. How do you feel about it now? Now write your name in different styles of script. Decide what each style says about you. Pick a partner to look at each style and tell you what it reveals about you.

Bring in a handwriting expert to analyze the writing.

Debrief. Discuss the exercise in the whole group. Is your name a handle? Do people make judgments about you based on your name? Does your signature illustrate your personality?

80 MEDITATION ON ME

This strategy by Jeffrey Shrank will help students focus on aspects of their personality as expressed in their language. In it, they are asked to think about themselves, make a self-description, clarify their own self-images, and determine what in that image they most value.

Before the activity, see that each student has eight small pieces of paper. Students should close their eyes, become comfortable, and let their minds play with words and phrases that describe themselves. Allow at least five minutes of quiet for this to happen. As in many of the experiences described here, the teacher should act as a participant in the activity.

When the group seems finished, have them open their eyes and write on eight pieces of paper the words and phrases that came to mind during the self-meditation. Tell them that these pieces of paper will not be for anyone but themselves

After the eight papers are filled, have students arrange them in order, putting the one they like best in the first position and the one they like least in the last. The other six should be ranked according to the degree of happiness or satisfaction they give.

Then have students spend some time with the word or phrase on each sheet of paper, fantasizing about it or recalling experiences they associate with the word. Caution them to take all the time they want with each word. Then encourage them to do whatever they wish with each piece of paper—throw it away, change it, give it to someone, or write on it.

After the experience the group can, if they are capable, share feelings during the exercise or do a written evaluation. An activity like this would be far less effective if performed out of context or simply to kill time or do something different. It is most effective in the context of a group or class where self-knowledge is recognized as a valid and deserved class activity.[6]

81   WHAT DO THE EYES TELL?

Give each student a magazine picture which shows only the eyes of a well-known person. Ask the student to write about the type of person the eyes suggest. Go around the room, with each student giving an oral biography of the person in the picture he or she has been given. Finally, tell who each pair of eyes belongs to.

Debrief. What do eyes alone tell us about a person? Were the students able to identify the people whose eyes were shown? Ask the students what they think people would say about them if they could see only their eyes.

---

82   RECIPE FOR A PERSON

Select partners. Ask each student to write a recipe for his or her partner. For example, "To make Mike, you need:

    short blond hair
    2 green eyes
    1 smiling mouth
    1 strong body
    1 pair torn, dirty tennis shoes

Comb hair and part in middle; let wind blow the hair. Place eyes in sunshine to get full twinkle effect. Add tennis shoes to the strong body, and mix in 10,000 freckles. Bake at the beach during a good surf. Do all this while laughing."

83   WHO IS YOUR SPECIAL FRIEND?

Give the following directions:

Lie on the floor and close your eyes. Think of a special friend. With eyes still closed, take a very close look at your friend. Pretend you and your friend are going to a special place. What type of place would be special for the two of you? What would you do at this special place? Take your time in visualizing it. Now take your friend's hand and walk him or her home. Walk back to your special place.

Sit up, open your eyes, and look at your friend if he or she is in the room. If you'd feel comfortable doing it, stand up, walk around the room, and tell each person; "I am (say your name) and my friend is (say your friend's name) and my friend (say what your friend does) for me."

Did you find it hard to see your friend with your eyes closed? Did you find it hard to tell everyone who your friend was? What does friendship mean? What responsibilities does friendship involve?

84   WHOM DO YOU RESPECT?

Join the class in this exercise:

Draw a ladder with ten rungs on it. On the top rung, put the name of the person you would most prefer to be like. On the bottom rung, put the person you would least prefer to be like. Place your own name on the ladder rung between the two where you feel it is most appropriate.

List five qualities of the person named on the top rung.

List five faults of the person named on the bottom rung.

List ten things you don't like about yourself. Of the ten, circle those you could not change even with very hard work.

Write yourself a plan of attack for changing the remaining items.

Debrief. Whose name was on the top rung? Why? Look at where you put your own name—do you think you were too hard on yourself? Did you realize that most things you didn't like about yourself could be changed if you really wanted to? Are you really trying to change them now? Do you basically like or dislike yourself?

85   CLOTHING AND PERSONALITY

Divide the class into groups of four. Give each student three sheets of paper bearing the following information:

Name: _____

Make notes on what each item says about a person.

1. shirt or blouse: _____

2. bottom apparel (pants, dress, shorts, or the like): _____

3. sweaters, coats: _____

4. jewelry (watches, rings, necklaces, headbands): _____

5. hairstyle:_____

6. shoes: _____

Students write their own names on each sheet and pass the sheets out to each member of the small group. Students complete the forms and return them to their owners. When all three sheets have been returned, each student writes a paragraph describing how he or she is being seen by others and several paragraphs about what he or she feels clothes have to say.[7]

---

[7]Adapted from *Values Clarification: A Handbook of Strategies for Teachers and Students* by Sidney B. Simon, Leland W. Howe, and Howard Kirschenbaum, copyright 1972 Hart Publishing Company, Inc.

Debrief. Is it preferable to feel comfortable as we are or to worry about how others see us? Why have clothes become a factor of personality? Ask the students if they care what their clothes say.

86 MAGIC SHOP

Explain sincerely to students that you once worked in a very unusual magic shop in San Francisco's Haight-Ashbury district. The magic shop was so unusual because in it you could buy such inanimate qualities as happiness, self-confidence, motivation, beauty, athletic ability, and so on. The shop was also unique in that the customers paid no cash for their purchases. They paid by giving something of themselves to the shop. A customer might, for example, order 10 percent more beauty; the shopkeeper might ask for 5 percent of that person's intelligence and 15 percent of his or her smile. Tell them that today the magic shop is open right in the classroom. Ask the students what percentage of what quality they want to buy and what percentage of what other quality they are willing to give up. If they don't know what to give up, tell them you'll make them an offer; and you will decide whether a deal is a good one. At the end of each deal, say, "Now you have _____ percent more _____."

Allow everyone who wants to buy something to do so. Next, have people buy something for someone else in the group. Finally, explain that the shop is having a sale; students can buy something for anyone (and they don't have to reveal who it is for) without giving up anything.

Debrief. Does the magic shop exist? Did everyone actually get what they purchased? Did some of the deals make people uncomfortable? Did the students not want some people to give up what they were giving up? Slowly the students should realize that the magic shop exists in everyone, that they can have most of the things they wished to purchase if they go after them.

87 WHAT DO I SEE IN THE MIRROR?

Divide the class into pairs. Give each dyad a mirror. One partner looks into the mirror and describes what he or she sees, while the other student listens. Then the partners reverse roles. All return to the large group. Each listener discusses the reactions of the viewing partner.

Debrief. Were the viewers comfortable? Could they be honest? Did they have to laugh to be confortable? Did they really stare into the mirror? Did they like what they saw?

88 IF I WERE AN ANIMAL, WHAT KIND WOULD I BE?

Students volunteer to go to the front of the class one by one. Class members interpret the personality of each student in front by responding to a series of questions asked by the teacher based on this question: "If (name of student) were an animal, what would he or she be?" Substitute other terms, such as: color, piece of cloth, instrument, food, place, clothing, flower, and others. The group then discusses what the answers revealed. The students in front of the class respond by sharing their feelings: Were they nervous? Did they see a consistency in the answers?

89 WHAT I AM

Students write down three things that they are—for example, honor student-basketball center-clarinet player; class president-sister-poet. Discuss the lists with the group. Allow time for students to question one another.

90 DEVELOPING MY PERSONALITY

Periodically during the year, have students develop lists of objectives or things to do. Suggested topics: People you like, people you hate, places you want to visit, things you'd like to learn, things you'd like to touch, traits you'd like to eliminate from your personality, and so on. Have students share parts of their lists with the group. Have them keep track of their lists and their accomplishments in their journals.

91   PASSING PEOPLE IN THE CIRCLE
AND GIVING HONEST PRAISE

Form groups of five or six. Each small group makes a very tight circle with one person in the middle. Remaining absolutely stiff, the person in the middle falls; those in the circle put their hands up to catch the middle person and gently pass him or her around the circle. The person in the middle keeps eyes closed and legs stiff, rotating on the heels. Those in the circle move the middle person very gently, keeping as many hands on his or her back as possible. Repeat until each student has been in the center.

Debrief. Did the students feel secure? Did they feel people cared about their safety? Did they like the sensations they experienced?

Now ask each student to take a turn in the middle, shaking hands with each person in the tight circle and saying something positive to each person: "I respect you because . . .," "I feel strongly about you because . . .," "I like the fact that you . . .," and so on. Once students take this exercise seriously, the outcome, based on all the previous personality exercises the class has done, will be deeply rewarding.[8]

Stay in the tight circles and debrief. How did each person feel? Whom did they feel close to? Why? Did they like what people said to them? Were they surprised?

92   TAPE-RECORDING THE VOICE

Have the students make brief recordings (about one minute long) of themselves reading something they have written. After studying their own voices, students write down what their voice indicates about them. Have students respond to each other's voices.

93   PICKING A PARTNER

Give students a list of things to do: Spend a day at beach, discuss a new idea, cuddle, study, and so on. Ask each student to write down the name of the person from the class with whom he or she would most

[8]Adapted from *Effective Communication* by Jeffrey Shrank, © 1971, Argus Communications, Niles, Illinois (cassette tape).

like to do this activity. Make the list so broad in scope that everyone in the class will be chosen for something. Go around the room, with each person reading the answer to each item. Anyone who is chosen can ask why he or she was chosen.

Debrief. Ask the students the following question: Why do you choose one person for one thing and another person for another thing? Were you surprised you were chosen for particular items? What does your surprise suggest?

94 PRESSURE: *SHOULD* AND *WANT*

Have students make a list of ten items that begin "I should _____."

Have students mark the items in the list that they would also include in a list of items that begin "I want to _____."

Debrief. Discuss why pressure exists to do certain things. Where does the pressure come from? Is the pressure helpful? Why, or why not? How much of the pressure arises because you want to accomplish the item and how much because others expect you to accomplish it?

95 PERSONAL PROBLEM SOLVING

Divide the group into trios. Within each trio, appoint one presenter, one helper, and one observer.

Each presenter takes about five minutes to present a personal problem (preferably not one of his or her own, but one about which the presenter feels strongly).

At the end of the presentation, the helper has ten minutes to ask questions and provide feedback, responses, suggestions, or comments. Then the presenter and the observer tell the helper which of the techniques used were of a helping nature and which were not. Discuss the whole exercise in the trios.

Debrief with the whole group. Did the helper moralize? Did the helper ask good questions? What body language did the helper use? What did his or her voice reveal? Did the helper maintain eye contact? Did the helper appear empathetic?

96   PLEASE HEAR WHAT I AM NOT SAYING

Pass out copies of the essay "Please Hear What I Am Not Saying" (see Appendix page 153), and discuss it with the class.

Debrief. What does the author mean by the term "game"? What is meant by the title? How does the author use the word "masks"? Ask the students to consider whether they play games or use masks.

6 Love/Marriage

Ask each student to write a definition of love. The student may not rely on quotes. Each definition must be original.

On the following day, ask each student to read his or her definition. List on the board any problems that occur in the definitions. The class may wish to choose the definition they like best or to combine several to come up with a composite definition.

Finally, ask the students to list the kinds and levels of love. Their list may include the following types of love:

mother-son
boyfriend-girlfriend
lover-lover
boy-girl
boy-boy
puppy
fascination
romantic
marriage-based
family-oriented
sexual, and others

Debrief. Discuss the meaning and importance of the listed types of love. Do we love "because . . . (you are handsome)," "if . . . (you would change)," or "even though . . . (you drink too much)"?

98 LOVE ADDICTION

Share with the students the article entitled "Interpersonal Heroin: Love Can Be an Addiction," from *Psychology Today* (August, 1974).

Debrief. Does love bring rights and responsibilities? Does love bring ownership? What is jealousy? Is jealousy healthy for a relationship? Is the problem *how* to love or *whom* to love? Is the process of love the process of finding an object to love at the best market price under the present conditions? Is it natural to want to love? Is love the joy of giving or receiving? What are the responsibilities of one who is in love? What is the "double standard," and why do we have it? Why do we often treat strangers more cordially than those we love? Is love a permanent emotion? Is marriage a logical step after romantic love? Is divorce the logical step when love dies?

99   LOVE ENDS: DIVORCE

Discuss the article entitled "Divorce Course," which is included in the Appendix, page 155.

Debrief. Ask the students the following questions: Would a course such as this be beneficial to your education? What do you think you would learn from such a course? What types of activities should we do in our course on this subject? How can we make the exercises as realistic as possible?

7 Death

Begin the unit on death with a discussion about different aspects of terminal illness. Discuss the following questions with the students: If you had a terminal illness and had a year or less to live, would you want to know? Do you feel you have the right to know? Would you want your friends to know? If you knew you were going to die would you change your lifestyle significantly? your morals? If you would choose to do a lot of things differently if you knew you were going to die, what is stopping you from doing them that way now?

Next, read a magazine article or newspaper account regarding a family who is living with a dying member. Role play the situation. How do the parents, the children, and outsiders (the doctor or priest, for example) confront the problem of death? Do they tell other family members? Do they tell the dying person? How does the family decide how it will act?

Discuss these questions with the students: Do you have as much right to die well as to live well? Do you have a responsibility to prevent death? Why does America view the aged as second-class citizens and prize youth and youthfulness?

Finally, read "A Story," by Jeri Doney[9], and discuss:

A Story

Once upon a time, not too many years ago, there was born into this world a baby girl. Her parents were proud and promised to raise her right. To make her independent and strong.

And while she was in the hospital nursery, she was afraid of the change and cried. And a nurse stroked her on the head and said, "Don't worry, little girl, everything will be all right."

And when she tried to roller-skate, but couldn't keep up with the other children, she cried in frustration. And her mother patted her on the head and said, "Don't worry, little girl, everything will be all right."

---

[9]Written when Jeri Doney was a senior in one of my classes.

And when she saw one man kill another, and cried in fear and confusion, her father patted her on the head and said, "Don't worry, little girl, everything will be all right."

And when she was confused by her growing up, she went to a "kindly soul" and tried to tell what was so strange to her; the "kindly soul" put on a smile, patted her on the head, and said, "Don't worry, little girl, everything will be all right."

And when the girl jumped from the bridge, she smiled and said, "Yes, *now* everything will be all right."

The End

101   DEATH: THE RELIGIOUS VIEW, THE MEDICAL VIEW

Invite a priest, rabbi, minister, or monk to talk to the class about how he or she deals with people who must face death in their families and to discuss the religious view of death he or she holds.

Invite a doctor to talk to the class about the medical view of death. Ask the doctor to discuss such questions as the prolonging of life, organ transplants, how he or she tells family members about death, and how he or she decides whom to tell.

Ask the doctor to arrange a class visit to a geriatrics ward. One doctor set up a very meaningful visit with a dying cancer patient who was most interested to speaking to our class about how he was facing the problem, how he viewed life and death, and how the students might think about death.

102   MY FUNERAL AND MY EPITAPH

Complete a unit on death by having students fantasize about their own funerals. Ask the students to close their eyes, relax, and visualize their own funerals. Guide them with questions: Who is attending? What kind of day is it? How are the people reacting? What kind of music is being played? Is the coffin open? How do you look? What did you die from?

Ask students to write their own epitaphs. Go around the room; those who wish to discuss their funerals or read their epitaphs may do so.

Students will often respond to this strategy in a humorous way. Throughout the discussion, help them to feel less embarrassed about confronting their feelings with regard to death in a serious way and to view death as an experience common to all life.

103   TRIP TO THE CEMETERY

Spend a day visiting a local cemetery. A very old one is most interesting. Sit in a circle, and debrief the experiences shared so far during the unit on death. Students will often share personal experiences of facing death in their own families. This strategy is often the most profitable and personally emotional experience of the death unit.

Have everyone run in the woods or along the beach or involve them in some heavy physical exercise after this day to work out all their emotions. On the following day, keep the class in a light mood. You may wish, for example, to ask them to write how they would spend an ideal forty-eight hours. Where would they go? What would they do? Who would go along? How much would it cost? What would they get out of it? This strategy returns their thoughts to life.

⑧ Loneliness

104 THE LONELY CADET

In 1971 Jim Pelosi, a cadet at the United States Military Academy, West Point, was convicted by the Student Honor Committee of cheating on a test. Pelosi, who had very high grades, denied cheating on the test, and witnesses supported his claim of innocence. Pelosi appealed the decision, and the case was dismissed. The Student Honor Committee, however, continued to believe that Pelosi was guilty and decided to subject him to the treatment known at the academy as The Silence.

The Silence requires that no one on campus speak to you, look at you, or even acknowledge your presence. Pelosi was not allowed to participate in any activities. During the first months of The Silence, he lost twenty-six pounds. Most cadets getting the silent treatment drop out of school, but Pelosi was determined to make the army his career and decided to stick it out; he remained at the school in silence for nineteen months.

West Pointers feel very strongly about their honor system; they want only honest leaders. The academy has a very long and proud tradition.

Ask the students to consider some of the following questions in light of Pelosi's story: Who was right and who wrong? Why? Would you have stayed at the academy? Does loneliness mean having no one around, or can you be lonely in a crowd? Why are you lonely?

Have some students volunteer for an isolation experience similar to the West Point Silence. Enlist friends, family, and schoolmates to participate in the experiment by asking them to ostracize the volunteers. (You may wish to introduce the term "ostracize" in class discussion.) After four days, have the volunteers report about their feelings. Ask them to imagine how they would feel if the situation were to continue for a year or for three years.

105   SELF-IMPOSED ISOLATION

Have all the students in the class stop all forms of communication for just one weekend—no television, no phone calls, no talking, no going out, no letter writing, no sign language. Have students report on their feelings and on whether they were able to stick it out for the whole two days.

106   WHAT MAKES ME LONELY?

Have students list the times, environments, and emotions that make them feel most lonely. Discuss ways of handling these times, places, and emotions. Are such feelings sometimes beneficial?

107   LONELINESS AND OLD AGE

Have students visit a home for the elderly, discuss the concept of loneliness with the residents, and report back to the class.

Ask them to befriend someone they think is lonely and report the experience to the class.

108   *ALONE* VERSUS *LONELY*

Suggest that students go off by themselves to camp, walk in the woods, sit by a stream. Was this time *alone* enjoyable? What is the difference between *alone* and *lonely*?

Social Problems

The strategies in this unit serve as a means of introducing, involving students in, or debriefing specific subject matter in sociology; many of them can fulfill more than one role. They are designed to "hook" students into seeing the importance, interest, or relevance of sociological themes in their own lives.

The themes are presented in no particular order, and are intended to be used in an order appropriate to your course of study. Many sociology, current events, or American government courses do not deal with all these topics. Researching techniques, values clarification, and problem-solving and decision-making skills are highly emphasized in this unit.

In Section XI, Social Service, students are encouraged to apply what they have learned to practical, field-experience strategies.

1 Discovering Problem Areas

109 SOCIAL PROBLEMS IN SONG

Play significant excerpts from songs by people (such as Buffy Sainte-Marie, Bob Dylan, Malvina Reynolds, Pete Seeger, Joan Baez, and others) who comment on different aspects of social problems. After students have listened to music for about forty-five minutes, ask them to list all the social problems that were sung about and to choose the three problems they feel are most significant. The class then will compile their lists of three and determine which three problems are the most significant to the group as a whole.

Debrief. How did the musicians deal with the problems? What were their views? What solutions did they suggest? What was the purpose of each one in doing the song?

Use the three problems the class has labeled most significant as the basis for study units.

110 SOCIAL SYMBOLS

Pass around pictures of familiar symbols—flags, the swastika, the ecology sign, the peace sign, the Star of David, various crosses, and others. Ask the students to write spontaneous reactions to the symbols using free association.

Then ask students to verbalize their responses. Did they see the element as a *symbol* or a *sign*? Discuss the differences in the two terms. (A rain cloud, for example, is a *sign* of rain; short lines on a weather map are a *symbol* for rain.) Do we react to symbols or signs? Do we react more violently to a policeman walking toward us with his night stick raised (sign) or to passing a police station (symbol). Do we react more actively to the passing of the American flag (symbol) or the passage of the 1964 Civil Rights Bill (sign)? Cite other examples of symbols and signs.

111   SOCIAL PROBLEMS MURAL

Roll out fifteen to twenty feet of butcher paper. Have students go through magazines and cut out pictures representing social problems. Have them paste the cutouts on the butcher paper to create a social problems mural.

112   CREATING A LIVING SOCIOGRAM

A sociogram is a diagram of circles on a large piece of paper, in which each circle represents a particular segment of the entire group. (The whole paper may represent the City of New York, for example, with circles representing the Blacks in the city, the Puerto Ricans, and so on.) Each circle is then connected to another with a straight line, indicating that some relationship exists between members of the two groups represented, although one group is not identical in all ways to the other group.

To develop an understanding of groups and subgroups, have a student make a visual sociogram by creating groups of students who hold hands to create circles. When the circles are appropriately distributed around the room, have the groups who have some relationship to each other show their connection: one member from each group will grab hands with a member the other in order to create a straight line that connects the groups. (Basketball players in one group might have a relationship with cheerleaders of another group). With the pattern still intact, debrief by discussing that student's placements of the others. Allow another student to make changes. Debrief that student's choices. Continue taking turns until most of the group is happy with the sociogram.

Do a final debriefing. Discuss what the students have learned. Were there many closed groups or lots of open groups? Were there enough groups for everyone? Did some students belong in more than one group? What kind of sociogram could we create for our school? for our city?

2 Poverty

113 WHAT IS POVERTY?

Have the class as a group determine an exact definition of "poor." "The Welfare Quagmire," a pamphlet published by the Urban League, is helpful in a discussion of myths, though it is dated. Assign students to visit the local welfare office, the state unemployment office, the food stamp office, and so on, to do some fact finding regarding the local definition of "poverty." Ask them to consider questions such as the following: Are most poor people working or unemployed? Do certain agencies determine the poverty level differently? Are most poor people Black? Are most Black people poor? What other groups are considered poor in your area? Is getting a job the main problem for the poor? Is poverty an accident of birth? What are local agencies doing about poverty?

After you and the students have done some fact finding and listened to local experts invited to talk to your class, try to define the problem of poverty in terms of how it affects poor youths. Next, suggest several alternative projects your class might do to lessen the effect of poverty on local youths. What things are local youths denied as a result of their poverty? What can your class do about the situation? They might, for example, conduct food drives at Thanksgiving and Christmas, pay fees for poor youths to recreational facilities, adopt a poor child or family. You may wish to arrange trips to a nearby poverty area to observe the visible problems.

114 EATING A POVERTY DIET

To develop an understanding of poverty, join the students in going on a poverty diet, spending no more than $1.50 per day per person for food. No cheating! Keep a record of what you eat and how you feel. Encourage the students to involve their families in the experiment. Take the money you have saved and send it to a poverty organization.

This strategy could lead into an entire unit on nutrition, health food, the use of preservatives in food, and other related topics.

115 PLAYING A POVERTY ROLE

Have students volunteer to dress "poorer." They may wish to visit other schools in the area and pretend to be new students. The "new" students might also sit in the cafeteria with an obviously meager lunch (such as chicken necks).

After a few days, students report back about the treatment they received as new "poor kids" in school.

3 Education

116 THE IRONY OF EDUCATION

Give each student a copy of the quote from Royce Van Norman and carry on a discussion in an effort to determine what the author was describing and the implications of the quote.

> It is not ironical that in a planned society of controlled workers given compulsory assignments, where religious expression is suppressed, the press controlled and all media of communication censored, where a puppet government is encouraged but denied any authority, where great attention is given to efficiency and character reports, and attendance at cultural assemblies is compulsory, where it is avowed that all will be administered to each according to his needs and performance required from each according to his abilities, and where those who flee are tracked down, returned and punished for trying to escape . . . we attempt to teach "the democratic system."

At the end of the discussion, complete the quote. The missing phrase, indicated by ellipses, is: "(in short in the milieu of the typical large American secondary school)."

117 WANT AD FOR A TEACHER

Have students write a want ad for a teacher they would most like to have. Compare their ad with the school district's job descriptions and advertisements.

118   A DAY AWAY FROM SCHOOL

Have students write down how they would spend a perfect day away from school and its teachers. Discuss how some of the things they have written could be done *during* school and *with* the teacher.

Debrief. Should school be a joyous place? Is having fun a legitimate objective of education?

119   ROLE PLAYING TO SOLVE AN EDUCATIONAL PROBLEM

Adapt the basic role-playing technique to a consideration of education by giving each class member a name tag: priest, principal, conservative parent, psychologist, student body president, Black Student Union president, teacher, Parent-Teacher Association president, department chairman, and the like.

Give each student a paper describing a school problem. Have them spend twenty minutes discussing the problem and how to solve it, from the point of view of the person described on their name tag. At the end of twenty minutes, have them pass their name tags to the person to their right and spend ten more minutes discussing the problem from their new role.

Debrief. Were the roles well represented? Was the problem realistic? Where was there blockage? Who helped?

120   CREATION OF A SCHOOL

An extensive and valuable educational project that teaches research, problem-solving, and communication skills is the creation of a new school plan. First students critique their school using the standards outlined in the Appendix. (See page 157). The score on the test will assist students in creating objectives and priorities for their new school. The students must then do some research: They may write letters to other schools, to the State Department of Education, to universities and other educational institutions; they may bring in education experts to testify before this "new school committee."

The class should then divide up into committees to deal with areas such as administration, curriculum, extra-curricular activities, grading, and whatever else the students are interested in.

Based upon their priorities and the research they have done, each committee will write a report on the problem it has considered, the possible solutions, and its ultimate recommendations. The committees must show awareness of the political and economic realities of the situation.

At this point the entire group should move into a committee of the whole to offer suggestions and propose amendments to the committee reports. When the final report is agreed upon and written, the committee should request that it be presented to the school board, the local press, the university School of Education, and others. Even if nothing changes, the students will have learned a great deal.

121   GRADES: WAD-JA-GET?

Pass out ditto copies of "Wad-Ja-Get?" (see Appendix, page 161.) Discuss the ramifications of the information it contains. Do some or all of the problems mentioned exist in your school? in your class? What can be done? What system of grading should this school adapt? this class? How can the present system be changed?

Discuss the question: If you were given a million dollars, would you continue to go to this school? any school? Why, or why not?

122   ALTERNATIVE EDUCATION PROGRAMS

Educational program alternatives can exist within the larger structure of the school. If staff and administration are creative, a student should not have to go to a separate institution or private free school to experience the joys of alternative innovative programming. Three programs that might be easily integrated into many school's structures are outlined below.

During *Spring Enrichment* or *Mini-Course Week,* all regular curricula are abandoned for a week. A new set of courses, suggested primarily by the students, is instituted. Specific program objectives might include:

1. To provide educational experience free of traditional evaluation (no grades are given).
2. To provide educational experiences that are not a part of the regular school curriculum.

3. To provide an opportunity for student/faculty involvement in curriculum planning and instruction.
4. To change the pace of the school routine during the spring.
5. To offer teachers an opportunity to teach in innovative ways.
6. To allow evaluation of the relationship between high-interest courses and class attendance.
7. To allow students to have fun at school.
8. To offer in-depth exploration into subjects covered only generally in regular classes.
9. To allow principles learned in the classroom to be put to use in promoting involvement and discovery outside the classroom.
10. To allow for opening new paths of communication between student and students, students and faculty, and faculty and faculty to facilitate ongoing curriculum planning and development.

A variety of approaches are possible; the one you decide upon will depend upon your financial and human resources. A student/faculty committee might draw up a list of possible courses and poll the students, who are to choose the final courses and offer additional suggestions. From this poll a curriculum may be set, instructors found, and rooms assigned. One possible format might include four 1½-hour classes per day for four days, with all-day and half-day classes on Friday. The longer Friday classes allow for field trips, related experiences, or extensions of the Monday–Thursday classes. All classes need not take place at school; small fees might be charged to cover expenses. Classes can cover any topic—from scuba diving to North American Indian poetry.

If you wish to involve students more fully in the planning process, you might select twelve or so students to be part of a *Mini-Course Class,* for which they receive a credit. Beginning early in the school year, the class meets for about three hours once every two weeks, working up to almost daily meetings during the week preceding Mini-Course Week. Minutes of the class meetings may be read in home rooms; the students in general can respond to developing plans by contacting their committee class representative.

First, the class must draw up a list of objectives for Mini-Course Week. Next, they may wish to survey nearby schools with innovative programs and research the literature regarding spring enrichment-type programs in other cities and states. The group may then wish to organize along the lines of a college, developing an organizational chart that delineates responsibilities. The principal, for instance, may become the college president, you may be the director of special projects, and students may fill other positions. A sample organizational chart suggests possible areas of responsibility:

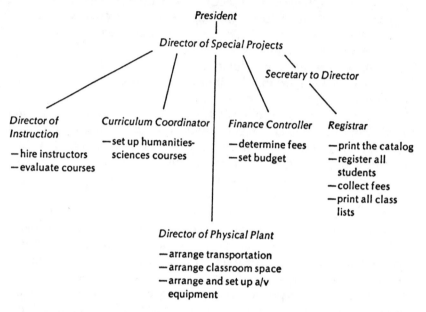

President

Director of Special Projects

Secretary to Director

Director of Instruction
—hire instructors
—evaluate courses

Curriculum Coordinator
—set up humanities-
   sciences courses

Finance Controller
—determine fees
—set budget

Registrar
—print the catalog
—register all
   students
—collect fees
—print all class
   lists

Director of Physical Plant
—arrange transportation
—arrange classroom space
—arrange and set up a/v
   equipment

While students help in all areas, they are primarily responsible for one specific area. With this approach, the major part of the learning will occur for the committee members. The committee devises the large list of class possibilities, and students select the final classes from that list.

Following the college organization gives students experience in reading a catalogue, setting up a class schedule, going through the registration procedure, paying fees, and finding and attending classes.

In keeping with the college theme, classes may vary in length, be offered from 8 A.M. to 8 P.M., and be taught whenever possible away from the school and by someone other than regular school staff. Regular teachers who are not teaching classes may serve as class monitors, taking roll and generally supervising. Mandatory attendance lends support to "hired staff" who prepare special courses; otherwise, half the class may not show up. The irregular hours allow college instructors or business people to participate as faculty and require students to determine their class hours and budget their free time.

Credit hours may be assigned to each class Monday–Thursday (one credit for every class hour). Establish a minimum requirement— perhaps four credits, plus one class on Friday—but allow students to take as many credits as they want.

Students print (or ditto) the catalog and distribute it. List fees. In one school which implemented this program there was a 10¢ per credit standard fee and some courses had additional fees. Gourmet cooking was $10, flying was $10, ceramics was $5. The most a student had to spend was 40¢; some students spent over $25.

Registration may be held during school hours on a first-come, first-served basis. Courses numbered 100–109 have sign-up sheets at one table, those numbered 110–119 at another table, and so on. Thus a student may register first at the table carrying his or her highest priority class. Students experience the same registration problems they would at any large college or university. They may have to rearrange a schedule because a class is closed, discover that checks for fees were not made out properly, or have the registrar tell them of a class-time conflict.

The courses may include such studies as car and motorcycle repair, crafts, college experience (where students go to sororities and fraternities at a nearby college and are assigned a big brother or big sister with whom they attend classes for the week), film making, operation of firearms, fishing and fly tying, gourmet cooking (taught by the cooks of local restaurants), guitar, ham radio, hang gliding, horsemanship, altered states of consciousness, photography, pilot training, psychology, professional work experience (students may spend time riding with the police or working in a bank or alongside a veterinarian), scuba diving (this class may be held in a pool), ski trip, story telling (students who sign up may spend the week at the public library telling stories to small children), swimming, rock music, gymnastics (or some other physical activity for which the school has no program), chess tournament, wilderness survival (which may include several days in the wilderness), and school maintenance (a program designed for those who skip or cause trouble during the week).

At one school where I used this program, less than five hundred dollars per year from the school's general fund had previously been applied to a Mini-Course Week. The year the student committee ran the program, we spent over one thousand dollars providing services to the students. But with a 10¢ tuition fee per credit and special fees for the classes that required materials or equipment, the school had to come up with only $90.10. We felt that we had offered ten times the product at less than one-fifth the cost. There was considerable interest in adding many of the courses to the regular curriculum.

Another special project that serves as an extension of the classroom is a *Lower Grades Tutorial Program*. Students volunteer to tutor several hours a week at a local grade school or junior high. Besides allowing students to experience a helping relationship, the program also helps them realize that other students also have learning problems — a realization that leads to a better understanding of teacher/student relationships. Surprisingly, the poorest students often turn out to be the best tutors, and the better they perform and the longer they tutor, the greater is the improvement in their own grades.

Another classroom expansion possiblity is a *School Exchange Workshop,* which you may develop in cooperation with an innovative teacher from another school. If, for example, you are both working on social problems in your classes, you may decide to bring the students together for a workshop on Social Problem Solving. The workshop may present many facets of social concern, from race to education. The goal of the workshop is to define problems, to suggest possible solutions, and, finally, to choose a course of action to solve the problem. You may wish to follow the session with a group debriefing and perhaps a potluck dinner, complete with entertainment.

One session of the workshop should take place at each school (one of my classes traveled 210 miles to participate in the exchange). The second session might explore aspects of the counter-culture — and may be led by resource people from a nearby university. Through this strategy, students coming from different mental and physical spaces are able to communicate with one other on subjects that affect them. The communication techniques learned, the substantive knowledge that is acquired, and the friends who are made make the exchange worthwhile.

Another exchange effort might involve taking four or five students to another school to conduct a workshop that explains some of the techniques, simulations, and strategies your class is using in the classroom. Such a give-and-take exchange will develop a sense of pride and self-confidence in your students and allow them to develop their communicative skills in a beneficial way.

123   SUGGESTIONS FOR IMPROVING
THE EDUCATIONAL SYSTEM

Listed below are sixteen suggestions from Neil Postman and Charles Weingartner's book, *Teaching as a Subversive Activity:*

1. Declare a five-year moratorium on the use of textbooks.

2. Have English teachers teach math, and math teachers teach English; have social studies teachers teach science, and science teachers teach art, and so on.

3. Transfer all the elementary school teachers to the high school, and vice versa.

4. Require every teacher who thinks he or she knows a subject well to write a book on that subject.

5. Dissolve all "subjects," "courses," and especially "course requirements."

6. Limit each teacher to three declarative and fifteen interrogative sentences per class.

7. Prohibit teachers from asking any questions to which they already know the answers.

8. Declare a moratorium on all tests and grades.

9. Require all teachers to undergo some form of psychotherapy as part of their in-service training.

10. Classify teachers according to their ability and make the lists public. Include teacher's IQs and reading scores, and note those who are culturally disadvantaged.

11. Require all teachers to take a test, prepared by students, on what the students know.

12. Make every class an elective, and withhold a teacher's monthly check if his or her students do not show any interest in going to next month's classes.

13. Require every teacher to take a one-year leave of absence every fourth year to work in some field other than education.

14. Require each teacher to provide some sort of evidence that he or she has had a loving relationship with at least one other human being.

15. Require that all graffiti accumulated in the school toilets be reproduced on large paper and hung in the school halls.

16. Issue a general prohibition against the use of the following words or phrases: *teach, syllabus, cover ground, IQ, make-up, test, disadvantaged, gifted, accelerated, enhancement, course, grade, score, human nature, dumb, college material,* and *administrative necessity.*[1]

---

[1]Adapted from *Teaching as A Subversive Activity* by Neil Postman and Charles Weingartner. Copyright © 1969 by Neil Postman and Charles Weingartner. Used by permission of the publisher, Delacorte Press.

Have students study the list to determine which suggestions they feel are worth pursuing. Have them develop plans of attack for getting the new approaches adopted.

Debrief. Which of the suggestions need student support? faculty support? administrative support? school board support? Which would require changes in policies and procedures? Which are illegal? Could the intended changes still be achieved if compromises were made with regard to the suggestions? Which of these items should be your first priority? Which of the items deserve priority? Which can be adopted only by the teacher?

124   IS SCHOOL MAKING YOU AVERAGE?

Ask the students to read the following poem:

I don't cause teachers trouble.
My grades have been okay.
I listen in my classes,
And I'm in school every day.
My teachers say I'm average
My parents think so too.
I wish I didn't know that,
'Cause there's lots I'd like to do.
I'd like to build a rocket.
I've a book that tells you how;
and start a stamp collection;
Well, no use in trying now.
'Cause since I found I'm average
I'm just smart enough to see
It means there's nothing special
That I should expect of me.

—Anonymous

Have them discuss the poem not only in light of themselves but in terms of whether the educational system is indeed breeding mediocrity and stifling creativity.

125   STUDENT EVALUATIONS OF TEACHERS

This exercise can be used in your own classroom or as a schoolwide project. Students will develop what they feel is a fair tool to measure the effectiveness of a teacher, a department, or the school.

Establish first whether the students feel a need for this project. Do they want to evaluate you? the department? the school? Do they want to publish their results? Do they want to provide information, or are they out to "get" some teacher?

Then direct the students to develop the evaluative tool and test it, gathering their information objectively and accurately and presenting their findings without bias.

Some possible measurement methods include:

Devise a tool that uses the evaluative words never, seldom, occasionally, most of the time, *and* always.[2] Students compile a list of statements which describe desirable qualities (including such items as: you make the subject interesting, you give enough time to do assignments, you are willing to give extra help, you exercise the correct amount of discipline). Students then use the list to evaluate the teacher by writing the appropriate word following each item. The total number of responses to each quality is then tallied and reported.

Devise a tool similar to the one described above that uses a numerical system of evaluation. Students compile a list of statements designed to describe an effective teacher and are asked to assign a numerical value (1–5) to each statement. The number 1 indicates *describes my teacher very well;* 2 indicates *describes my teacher most of the time;* 3 indicates *describes my teacher about half the time;* 4 indicates *describes my teacher occasionally or seldom;* 5 indicates *describes my teacher not at all.* Totals are then computed, and an average score for each item is reported.[3]

Design a tool that allows students to give more definitive responses to a list of items designed to describe an effective teacher. Students are asked to respond to a list of items, all of which begin, "In this class, the teacher generally . . . ." Students respond *yes, no,* or *don't know.* Items include such statements as *knows my interest, knows when I need help, uses teaching methods that make me want to learn.* The percen-

---

[2]Adapted from "Should Students Evaluate Teachers?" by Joan Jacobson, *Today's Education,* May, 1973, with the permission of the author and the publisher. Copyright © 1973 by National Education Association.

[3]Suggested in Rogee's "Style of Teaching Inventory."

tage of *yes, no,* and *don't know* responses are tabulated and recorded for each statement.

Teachers seeking a qualitative evaluation requiring more detailed student response may ask the students to write their responses to four simple questions:

This class has been of greatest help to me because . . .
This class has failed me because . . .
My recommendations for the class are . . .
My grade in the class was . . .

Typical and enlightening responses are reported to each of the teacher's classes.

Design a tool that separates out certain topics (such as grading) *for judgment.* A topic is selected, and some general questions about the teacher's abilities with regard to the topic are listed: Have I been willing to listen to your side? Have I been fair? Have I been willing to assign make-up work? Have I given tests that measured your learning? Below this set of questions appear the following terms: excellent-5; good-4; fair-3; adequate-2; and poor-1. Students are to circle one response which evaluates the teacher with regard to the selected topic. The teacher's score is tabulated, averaged, and reported to the class or student body.

A similar tool may be designed that allows more precise evaluation. An area of concern such as "course organization" is selected. A numerical evaluation of the teacher's skill in the area of concern is devised.

Values of 1–3 indicate *carefully planned, well organized.* Values of 4–6 indicate *some organization; not always clear.* Values of 7–9 indicate *lacks organization and planning.* Students merely choose the number that best fits their evaluation of the teacher in each area of concern. Percentages are computed and recorded.[4]

An information-type evaluation might also be tried. It might include such items as: Does the teacher give pop quizzes? Is outside reading assigned? Does the teacher give subjective or objective tests? Is a term paper a course requirement? Does the teacher grade on the curve? Does he or she primarily lecture or make use of discussion? Does the teacher rely heavily on the textbook? From their responses to these and similar questions, students can draw their own conclusions.

---

[4]Used at San Mateo High School, San Mateo, California.

126   TEACHER'S DESIRABLE CHARACTERISTICS

Students at San Mateo Alternative Learning Laboratory developed a list of twenty-five characteristics they felt desirable in order for a teacher to be an effective instructor. The list was then distributed to groups of students and to groups of student teachers who were asked to select the ten most desirable characteristics. The results were informative; the lists compiled by the two groups mentioned very few of the same characteristics and ranked them differently.

Student Teacher List

1. knowledge of subject matter
2. formality, sophistication
3. ability to discipline
4. interest in subject
5. high IQ
6. ability to motivate students
7. a social background that relates to the classroom situation
8. ability to explain well
9. ability to get along well with others
10. courage, self-confidence

Student List

1. interest in students as individuals
2. patience, willingness to repeat
3. fairness
4. explains things clearly
5. humorous
6. open-minded
7. informal; does not feel superior
8. interest in subject
9. neat appearance
10. knowledge of subject matter

Have your students develop a list and distribute it to other students and teachers in your school. Compare your results with those of the San Mateo students. Discuss.

4 Race and Prejudice

127 RACE QUIZ

Have students answer the following questions on a piece of paper, and then discuss the "correct" answers.

1. What color is God?
2. What color is flesh, or a skin-colored band-aid?
3. What is beautiful, and what is ugly?
4. Name three things beginning with black that are of a positive nature (*not* "black Sunday," "Black Death," "black of night," "black witch," and the like).

128 PREJUDICE QUIZ

Have students answer the following questions. Then discuss the reasons for the true and false answers.

1. When Blacks move into an area, property values *initially* go down.

2. Certain physical characteristics make it possible to distinguish criminal types.

3. People marry merely to make their children legitimate.

4. It has been proven that Aryan peoples are superior both physically and mentally to other peoples.

5. Every American wants the most pressing social issues to be solved.

6. Poverty is merely being without a job and money.

7. Only one-half of the people who qualify for welfare are on the welfare rolls.

8. Only one-half the people on welfare rolls are actually employable.

9. Most Blacks are poor.

10. Most poor people are Blacks.

11. Some people have inborn prejudices.

12. Prejudices are largely unconscious.

13. Prejudice is learned by being near those whom you are prejudiced against.

14. One attaches prejudice to groups, not to individuals.

15. People enjoy being prejudiced.

16. The position of minorities in America is the result of their own laziness, shiftlessness, over-aggression, and over-ambition.

17. Minorities like the position that they are in. They are most content in that position.

18. Discrimination actually benefits minorities. They receive plenty of welfare.

19. Minority people are against integration—they like being with their own kind.

20. Irish, Italians, and Poles have worked their way up in this country. Blacks, American Indians, and Chicanos could too, if they wanted to.

21. Blacks are better off in America than in Africa, and Indians are better off on reservations.

22. We shouldn't get so upset about the problems of minorities. Whites have troubles too.

Answers:

1. (T) Property values *initially* go down, because some people are scared into moving and selling out cheap and fast. Often real estate people will generate the fear themselves in order to make a number of quick sales. Shortly, property values begin to rise again.

2. (F) We can't distinguish physical characteristics for criminal types. Some controversial research is being done on the extra chromosome syndrome, which some researchers hold may indicate aggressive and perhaps criminal behavior.

3. (F) In this society, people marry for more reasons than to have children legally; they also marry for spiritual, legal, emotional, and social reasons.

4. (F) While many researchers have tried, no one has proven one race to be superior over another. Writing tests that will measure intelligence without bias present a problem. An Eskimo may not know how to read and might do poorly in your school, but you might not survive too long in the Arctic either. So who is more intelligent?

5. (F) First, not everyone agrees as to what the social problems are. For example, with regard to unemployment, some people say the problem is that people won't work, whereas others say the problem is that no jobs are available. Secondly, many people make a lot of money from social problems—for example, drug pushers and social welfare agencies stay in business, the slum lord has lots of tenants, and so on.

6. (F) Most people who are poor work; poverty can be a state of mind. Your feelings about your economic position are very important to your attitude about poverty.

7. (T) Many people don't know welfare exists, many are too proud to apply, and some don't feel it is worth the trouble and paper work.

8. (T) Most people on welfare rolls are handicapped to the point of being unemployable or minimally employable, or are women who are heads of households and thus kept at home to care for children.

9. (T) Over 50 percent of Blacks fall below the poverty line.

10. (F) Of all the people below the poverty line, most are white. Do you see the difference in this question and question 9?

11. (F) Prejudice is a learned behavior.

12. (F) Most people are fully aware that they are prejudiced.

13. (F) Most people who are prejudiced against a certain group do not live, work, or play with members of that group.

14. (T) To hate all Indians is much easier than to hate your mailman, who happens to be an Indian.

15. (T) Many people feel it is "in" or smart to voice feelings of prejudice.

16-22. These questions indicate fallacious thinking. Point out the contradictions, inaccurate information, or circular reasoning contained in the statements.

129 LOST LETTER

Have your students address and stamp ten letters to liberal organizations (you can make up liberal-sounding names, if you wish). Use the same address for each letter—perhaps the home address of one of the students. Address ten letters to super-conservative and patriotic organizations. Drop these "letters" in public places. See how many of each group are dropped in a mailbox by a kind citizen.[5]
Discuss which letters were mailed and which were not.

130 THE STATISTICAL INDIAN

Distribute copies of the following data concerning American Indians:

- ☐ The average infant mortality rate after the first month of life is three times the national average.
- ☐ The average life span of Indians is 44 years, nearly one-third short of the national average of 64 years.
- ☐ The Indians yearly income average, $1,500, is half the national poverty level.
- ☐ The Indians account for one-half of one percent of the population.
- ☐ The Indian bureaucracy—the Bureau of Indian Affairs—has now reached a ratio of one official to every eighteen Indians.
- ☐ At the Pine Ridge Reservation in South Dakota, the largest in the nation, $8,040 a year is spent per family to help them out of poverty, yet the median income among these Indians is only $1,910 per family.

☐ Suicides among Indian teenagers average three times the national rate; on some reservations the suicide rate has reached ten times the national average.

☐ The average Indian living under federal supervision has completed five years of school.

☐ Dropout rates on reservations are twice the national average.

☐ Indian children score consistently lower than white children at every grade level, in both verbal and nonverbal skills, according to national tests administered in 1965. The longer the Indian child stays in school, the further behind he or she gets.

☐ More than one out of five Indian males, or 23 percent, have not completed five years of school.

Debrief. Ask the students the following questions: Compare the quality of life of Indians to that of whites. Would you want to live on a reservation? If you did live on the reservation, what are the chances that your father would be alive? Your brothers and sisters? Do you think you would still be in school? Trace the historical events of the development of the reservations. As bad as the reservations are, the Indians don't want them abolished. Why?

131 INDIAN PARADOX

Read to the students the essay (see page 163 in the Appendix) that discusses the purchase of white lands by the Indians and the social changes that will follow the purchase—a satirical reversal of the existing situation.

Debrief. The essay is an example of political satire. What does satire mean? What does the UNA represent? What historical events are parodied in the first paragraph? List them, and similar events, on the board. Make a list of the problems the Indians are referring to in this paper. Present some possible solutions to these problems.

132 THE CHITTERLING TEST

The Chitterling Test, devised by Adrian Dove, a Black social worker from Watts, presupposes a familiarity with the Black subculture. A score of 11 or less indicates a less-than-acceptable knowledge—you are culturally deprived. Give your students the test, which is included in the Appendix (page 165).

Debrief. Discuss the merits of IQ tests. Take a poll to see how well the students did on this test. Did they feel it was a fair test of IQ? Is it fair to have standardized tests at all? What does testing prove?

133   CASE STUDIES: RACISM AND STEREOTYPING

Have white students go to local motels and hotels to determine rates for a family reunion. Have Black students do the same. Were they given different treatment?

Do Blacks get change counted into their hands or on the counter?

When you see an Indian leaning against a street lamp, do you automatically assume he is drunk?

If you have no direct experience with minority groups, invite guest speakers into the class to discuss the issues surrounding racial stereotyping and prejudicial treatment of minority group members.

134   COMMUNITY VOLUNTEER

Have students volunteer time to community projects or agencies that serve minority people.

5 Sports and Society

135 MALE/FEMALE ATHLETES

Discuss the following statement:

> Society cuts the penis off the male dancer and places it on the female athlete. — Dr. Marie Hart

Debrief. For decades the male dancer has been considered a sissy, when in reality he is probably the most highly tuned of physical athletes (see George Leonard's *The Ultimate Athlete* and James Michener's *Sports in America*). On the other hand, women athletes have always been considered tomboys or unfeminine. Why has society adopted these views?

136 POSITION PAPER: SPORTS AND SOCIETY

Have students research some of the suggested topics and bring back their research with the idea of the class developing a position paper, complete with background, problem statement, and recommendations on sports and society.

1. NCAA-AAU-Olympic Committee controversy
2. Blacks and sports
3. Violence in sports
4. Winning versus participation
5. Player's unions, reserve clause, Rozelle rule
6. Amateur athletes in the United States versus those in the Eastern European countries
7. Opportunities for women in sports
8. Expanding sports budgets
9. Value of the Olympics — nationalism in sports
10. Role of physical education in sports

11. Sports programs for everyone
12. College sports and college education
13. Why no Denver Olympics?
14. Life-long sports versus team sports

137   NEW GAMES

Have students read and then play some of the new games that George
Leonard explains in his book *The Ultimate Athlete.* Also see the book
New Games, published by the New Games Foundation.

Ask students to develop several of their own new games, using the
objectives of cooperation, maximum participation, and co-ed teams.
Hold a New Games Festival.

138   TITLE IX

Have students study Title IX of the 1972 Education Amendments Act,
which prohibits sexual discrimination in school programs, and determine the ramifications of it in your own school program.

139   HIGH SCHOOL ATHLETICS

Examine how the sociological concepts of race, sexism, violence,
culture, and nationalism are manifested in sports.

Consumer Education: Advertising/ Manipulation

6

Study the material included in the Appendix, adapted from Vance Packard's *The Hidden Persuaders.* (See page 169.)

Have students make a study of how an advertiser sells a particular product. Ask them to address themselves to the following questions: What market is the advertiser trying to reach (age, sex, type, income)? What image of the product is conveyed by the ad? What subtle ideas are reflected in the ad? (No women appear in the Marlboro cigarette commercials, and the actors do not talk; the Camel cigarette man always has his coat tossed over his shoulder, and so on.) Ask the students to write up their study results and present the reports to the class.

Debrief. Discuss whether or not Packard's research is outdated. In what way have advertisers changed their campaigns since Packard's book was written in 1957? What social, cultural, and economic events have brought about changes in advertising?

141 SELLING A PRODUCT

Have the class devise an advertising campaign to sell the school a product that does not exist, such as the Gnihton ("nothing" spelled backwards).

Debrief. Can one, through an effective campaign, get people to pledge money to buy something that they haven't seen and that does not exist? Discuss the implications of this project in terms of political campaigns. You may want to watch the film *The Selling of the President* and discuss the "Kennedy image."

7 Closing the Generation Gap

Generation Gap Night is an attempt to introduce parents to some of the activities that their children have been exposed to in the regular classroom. Here is one program:

1. *Introduction.* The teacher or a student makes some explanatory remarks.

2. *Introductory Warm-up Activities.* The students choose those strategies they have enjoyed most and do them with the parents. Encourage students to relate to parents other than their own.

3. *Opening Lines of Communication.* Students choose their favorite nonverbal and verbal strategy to warm up the group, and again relate to the parents of other students rather than to their own.

4. *The Issues.* Have the students do Strategy 143 with their own parents.

5. *Bill of Rights.* Divide the group into parents and students. Ask the parents to work on a Parents' Bill of Rights and the students to work on a Students' Bill of Rights (see samples in the Appendix beginning on page 173). Each group then reads its Bill of Rights to the other group and answers questions in defense of its bill. Each group will then select the three most important rights from its bill. Redivide the class into three equal groups containing both students and parents. Each group discusses a pair of items—one from each of the original two groups—and determines how these two items need not be mutually exclusive but can be compatible. Each group then reports to the whole group.

6. *Communication.* Divide the group into small groups of four parents and four to six students. Ask each group to read and discuss "How to Ruin Your Children" and "If a Child Lives With . . . the Child Learns . . ." (in the Appendix), arriving at an answer for parents and

teenagers in general and for the specific parents or teenagers. Then have them take the Reach Quiz (in the Appendix). This material has been so universally reproduced that its original source has been lost.

7. *Film.* Show one of the generation gap films recommended in the bibliography. Discuss the film.

8. *Debriefing and Open Question Session.* Some of the quotes you might use as a basis for discussion include these from Margaret Mead's *Culture and Commitment:*

> In the past it was "What shall I commit my life to?" Now it is "Is there anything worth committing my life to as the world presently exists?"

> Elders say "I have been young and you have never been old." But today's young people respond, "But you have never been young in the world I am young in and you never can be."

Communication is a dialogue. In order for dialogue to take place, you must have a common vocabulary. Do youth and elders have a common vocabulary? Or is their communication like two television sets that have been turned on and are facing each other?

143 PARENT'S VIEW/STUDENT'S VIEW

In the generation gap, the alienation of elders is often overlooked at the expense of the alienation of youth. Have the students and parents fill in the blanks:

(Students) My parents feel that _____ should be the most important thing to me. I feel that _____ is really most important.

(Parents) I feel _____ is most important for my son or daughter. I believe he or she feels that _____ is most important.

Discuss the answers.

8 Violence

144 VIOLENT FANTASIES

Have students lie down and relax. Have them each imagine themselves to be animals walking through the forest or jungle or some other landscape. Have them imagine the person they most hate as another animal and imagine that animal to be walking toward them. Take about ten minutes for the fantasy of what will happen when the two animals meet.

Have each student discuss his or her fantasy. Did one animal flee? Did a fight take place? How did the fight end? Did the students stop their fantasies abruptly if they became uncomfortable? How do they feel now that the fantasy is over? Is violence a good thing to think about?

145 PICTURES OF VIOLENCE

Show students pictures of violence from magazines and have them respond on paper by free association.

Discuss their responses. Are human beings basically violent? Is violence learned? Is this generation more violent than the last? You may wish to supplement your discussion with some of the thoughts of Robert Ardrey, who has written widely on animal behavior. Does frustration lead to violence? How do we handle frustration? How do we eliminate violence? Is poverty violent? Is racism?

146 VIOLENCE ON TELEVISION

Have students study violence on television. When does it occur, how, how often, in what form, and what is the effect? How does the violence on the news compare with the violence in other programs? Are the cartoon series violent? What does "the family hour" really mean? Why does kissing a breast earn an "X" rating but stabbing a breast earn a "PG" rating?

147 WHO IS THE MOST VIOLENT?

Read the following poem by Julius Lester from *Search for a New Land.*[6]

Linda failed to return home from a dance Friday night.
On Saturday
she admitted she had spent the night
with an Air Force lieutenant.
The Pratts decided on a punishment
that would "wake Linda up."
They ordered her to shoot the dog
she had owned about two years.
On Sunday,
the Pratts and
Linda
took the dog into the desert
near their home.
They had the girl
dig a shallow grave.
Then
Mrs. Pratt grasped the dog between her hands and
Mr. Pratt
gave his daughter
a .22 caliber pistol
and told her
to shoot the dog.
Instead,
the girl
put the pistol
to her right temple
and shot herself.
The police said
there were no charges
that could be filed
against the parents
except possibly
cruelty
to animals.

Have the students take the following multiple-choice test:
The most violent persons in this true story were:

a. Linda, who slept with the lieutenant and pulled the trigger.
b. The Air Force lieutenant who took advantage of Linda.
c. Mr. and Mrs. Pratt, who ordered the dog shot.
d. The police, who could find no charges to be filed.
e. The dog.
f. The society, which permitted this to happen and offered no corrective action.

Discuss the students' responses.

148   VIOLENT CRIMES

Discuss the following quote:

> The public fears most those crimes which occur least often. One is more likely to be victimized by a "friend" or relative than a stranger. The closer the relationship, the greater the hazard. In one sense the greatest threat to anyone is himself, since suicides are more than twice as common as homocides.
>
> — *Jeffrey Shrank*

This unit on violence could include discussions of rape or suicide, involving community experts on all facets of the problems.

9 Women's Liberation

149 SEXIST RIDDLE

Ask students to answer this riddle: A man is driving with his son on the freeway. They are involved in an accident. The boy is taken to the hospital. In the examining room, the surgeon says, "I can't operate on this boy; he is my son.

Answer: The surgeon is the boy's mother.

Debrief. Ask the students: What assumptions did you make? Are you a sexist?

150 MASCULINE/FEMININE

Give students a list of words. Have them mark each word as being masculine (M) or feminine (F). Use words that are normally stereotypical, such as: honey, pretty, strong, sensitive, religious, petty, athletic, and so on.

Do certain words connote male or female attributes? Is limiting them to a specific connotation sexist? Discuss other words or phrases and the attitudes their usage implies.

151 SEXISM IN THE MEDIA

Have students listen to the radio, watch television, look through magazines for examples of sexist ads. Discuss the ads in class. You might want to point out *Ms.* magazine's section called "No Comment," in which sexist ads submitted by readers are reprinted.

152   INFERIOR/SUPERIOR

Jeffrey Shrank forces students to realize their sexism in this strategy:

Detecting Sexism in the Group

Distribute a questionnaire with about four or five different items to be evaluated. Each item is a very brief description of a person, from which the person filling out the questionnaire is expected to draw tentative conclusions. The questionnaire is presented as a test in evaluating people on the basis of incomplete information. No mention should be made of sexism.

Half the group (or half of the groups) receives the questionnaire, while the other half is given a questionnaire identical in all respects, except that the names are changed from one sex to the other. While half the class is evaluating a candy company executive named John, the other half is judging the same executive, this time named Joan. The existence of two questionnaires should not be revealed before they are completed. The questionnaires are then evaluated by comparing the total of the responses of those who had the male names to those who had female names. Discussion follows the tabulation.

Here is one sample questionnaire. Remember to prepare a second version with each name changed to indicate the opposite sex.

Evaluations Based on Incomplete Information

From the limited information given about each person below, you are to make an educated guess as to some of that person's character traits.

Encircle one number on the rating scale; there are no right and wrong answers in this test.

1. John works at Bell Telephone Company, is married and has two children. He wears colorful clothes. He probably is:

INTELLIGENT	1 2 3 4 5	STUPID
COMPETENT	1 2 3 4 5	INCOMPETENT
RATIONAL	1 2 3 4 5	EMOTIONAL

2. Ruth is 18 years old and a sophomore college student. She is five feet, eight inches tall and has blond hair. She makes average grades and dates about once a week. She probably is:

ARTISTIC	1 2 3 4 5	SCIENTIFIC
AGGRESSIVE	1 2 3 4 5	PASSIVE
INDEPENDENT	1 2 3 4 5	DEPENDENT

3. James Day is 46 years old, a professional writer, is married and has three children. His wife also works, and they own their own home. He probably is:

SELF-CENTERED	1	2	3	4	5	OTHER-CENTERED
ATTRACTIVE	1	2	3	4	5	UNATTRACTIVE
CONTENT	1	2	3	4	5	AMBITIOUS

The questionnaire can be left with only three items to mark or could be expanded to six by composing three more descriptions but using the same eighteen descriptive adjectives.[7]

153   MALE/FEMALE VALUES

Read the following story to the class. Have students keep a list of characters. After hearing the story, they are to rate the characters in the order of those they *dislike the most*. Discuss their choices.

Once upon a time, a woman named Abigail was in love with a man named Gregory. Gregory lived on the far shore of the river. Abigail lived on the opposite shore of the river. The river which separated the two lovers was teeming with man-eating alligators. Abigail wanted to cross the river to be with Gregory. Unfortunately, the bridge had been washed out. So she went to ask Sinbad, a riverboat captain, to take her across. He said he would be glad to, if she would consent to go to bed with him preceding the voyage. She promptly refused and went to a friend named Ivan to explain her plight. Ivan did not want to be involved at all in the situation. Abigail felt her only alternative was to accept Sinbad's terms. Sinbad fulfilled his promise to Abigail and delivered her into the arms of Gregory.

When she told Gregory about her amorous escapade in order to cross the river, Gregory cast her aside with disdain. Heartsick and dejected, Abigail turned to Slug with her tale of woe. Slug, feeling compassion for Abigail, sought out Gregory and beat him brutally. Abigail was overjoyed at the sign of Gregory getting his due. As the sun sets on the horizon, we hear Abigail laughing at Gregory.[8]

---

[7]From *Teaching Human Beings: 101 Subversive Activities for the Classroom.* Copyright © 1972 by Jeffrey Shrank. Reprinted by permission of Beacon Press.

[8]From *Values Clarification: A Handbook of Strategies for Teachers and Students* by Sidney B. Simon, Leland W. Howe, and Howard Kirschenbaum, copyright 1972 Hart Publishing Company, Inc.

Debrief. Upon what criteria did you base your decisions? Were your decisions based on sexual stereotypes, morals, emotions, logic, or some other criteria? Did the males vote differently from the females?

154   WOMEN'S LIBERATION TEST

Have students answer the following questions. Then compare the responses of boys and girls on each question.

1. To have children is a natural desire for women.
2. The mother instinct is biological in human females.
3. There is no double standard with regard to sex.
4. Women should be virgins at marriage.
5. It is better that men are not virgins at the time of marriage.
6. Women are more emotional than men.
7. Some jobs are better suited for men.
8. "I don't mind working with women, but I don't want a woman boss."
9. Women in athletics are mediocre in terms of ability.
10. Men need to learn to cry.

155   DISCUSSION ABOUT THE WOMEN'S LIBERATION MOVEMENT

Discuss the following questions with your class:

1. Are women demanding a society that is similar in structure and systems to the present men's society, or are they seeking a new society based upon a nonsexual orientation? Is it more beneficial for children to be around their mothers or around other children? (Discuss the concept of working mothers.) What does it mean to be a man? a woman? Are men more emotional than women? What is women's liberation, and what isn't? Does liberating women restrict or liberate men?
2. Does the women's movement have a masculine orientation? For example, why do women demand the use of Ms. rather than suggesting a Mrs.-type label for married men? Are women accepting male values by pursuing traditionally male goals such as executive status, political office and so on? Are women demanding men's

roles rather than demanding that men be allowed equal opportunity to become nurses, secretaries, or to fulfill other roles stereotyped as "women's roles"? Are they suggesting that athletic scholarships also be given to women rather than that none be given? What do men have to gain or lose with women's liberation? What does the Equal Rights Amendment mean in terms of social change?

3. Are girls more outgoing in social settings than boys? Do girls lack the motivation for achievement? Are girls better at memorization and boys better at abstract thinking? Do girls have a poorer concept of themselves than boys?

4. Are boys more aggressive than girls? Why do boys test better in math and girls in verbal skills on the American College Test (ACT) and the Scholastic Aptitude Test (SAT)? Are boys more dominant in relationships than girls? Are boys more competitive than girls? Are men or women better equipped to raise children?

10 Career Education

156 THE VISITING GRADUATES

Invite recently graduated alumni to return to your school for a give-and-take seminar about transition problems of leaving high school for college, work, service, travel, and/or marriage.

157 TALENT BANK

Have your students develop a catalogue of human resources in your community in government, business, social services, professional services, labor. Those people listed in the talent bank should be willing to meet with the class or with individual students to talk about their careers, or to take students on field trips of their places of work, and/or to place students in jobs within their organizations.

158 DEVELOPING A CAREER PLAN

Have each student write a want ad for what he or she considers to be the perfect job. Have them use want ad language and include qualifications, responsibilities, benefits, salary, hours, and so on.

Next, students should consult the want ad section of a large newspaper to find ads for jobs in their areas of interest and to compare their own ads with those they find in the paper. If no ads are listed, this discovery, too, should be informative.

Have them contact the personnel director of establishments that hire people in their areas of interest to ask how many people have been hired in the last year; the last five years. At what level, at what salaries, and with what qualifications have these people been hired?

Each student will then visit the establishment and view as many levels of the working structure as possible. If an interview can be set up, so much the better. The student should at least meet with the personnel director. Have the students make written reports of their visits.

The student then needs to develop a realistic plan for acquiring the dream job. How much education is needed (college, vocational school, union training, apprenticeship, professional school)? Would volunteer work help one to secure a job? Whatever the avenue of education, have the student investigate the options of where this education could be acquired. Have the student determine how long it would take to acquire this education, and how much it would cost.

Next have students explore what alternatives are open to them if the jobs specifically prepared for were eliminated. What else could they do? (One who has trained to be a teacher could also be a textbook editor, a school supplies salesman, an administrator, a librarian.) Students should list as many related options as possible and report on additional training or other requisites for them.

Complete this whole process for at least three jobs. Then see if at least three hours a week of volunteer or observation work could be set up with the establishment in which each student is most interested.

11 Futurism

159 USING THE SCHOOL MEDIA

If your school has an intercom system or a video recorder, you have the tools to present "specials" on topics your class is studying, to do news programs, or to use the equipment as the medium for school communication. Both the media themselves and the subject content become areas of study.

160 TECHNOLOGICAL DEVELOPMENT

After viewing two films—Marshall McLuhan's *The Medium Is the Massage* and Alvin Toffler's *Future Shock*—have students list side-by-side the advantages and disadvantages of technological developments.

161 TECHNOLOGY THEN AND NOW

Have students make a list of all the electrical appliances and forms of entertainment available to them today and take the list to their parents to see how many of the items were available when they were in high school.

Debrief. What changes have been made in the items that were available? Have the new items made your parents happier, less happy, or neither? What other impacts do they feel these innovations have had on their lives?

162 FUTURISM AND POPULATION

Propose to students that conceiving the world's entire population is a problem which can be solved by "compressing" the earth's population to a representative 1,000. Have students develop a profile of the make-up of the 1,000 using whatever resources they can think of. Then compare their profile to the following accurate composite:

> Of the 1,000, 305 people are white, 695 are nonwhite; 60 are American, 64 are Russians, 225 are Chinese Communists. The 60 Americans have nearly half the total income, with the other 940 sharing the other half. The 60 Americans have an average life expectancy of 70 years, while all others can expect to live less than 40 years. The Americans have up to now had 10 times as much to eat per person as all the rest of the people. The Americans produce 16 percent of the world's total food supply, eat all but 1/2 percent, and keep part of that for future use. More than 400 people cannot read or write. Of the 1,000, 330 people are Christian, while 670 either belong to other faiths—Jewish, Hindu, Buddhist, and so on—or have no formal religious beliefs. Of the 1,000, 320 people live on land controlled by communists. More than half the group have never heard of Christ, while more than half have heard of Marx.

After you have discussed this composite profile, tell the students that beings with greatly advanced intelligence from another planet have decided to take this 1,000-member group (represented by the class) to another planet to live. The group must decide unanimously whether they wish to (1) begin all over again to build a civilization, in which case the beings from the other planet will erase their *total memory*, including language, or (2) remember all that they are and all that has been accomplished on Earth and build from that.

Debrief. Would it be preferable to enter the new world with no memory of war, racism, sexism, population problems, and so on, or would Earth experiences prove helpful in resolving these problems should they arise?

163 HOW SIGNIFICANT ARE YOU?

Read the class the story "The Ant," written by Jeffrey Shrank.

> One day an ant was assigned his first task outside the anthill. He was told to drag back a dead grasshopper killed by the elders in a raid the previous day.

Out went our young hero. Upon exiting from the anthill, he was profoundly impressed and even shocked at the size of the outside world. He had heard tales that the world was larger than his own world, but never had he experienced such massive size.

At once he scurried in search of the grasshopper. As he continued his search, carefully following the directions, he came to a barrier that he could not surmount. So he did what any good ant would do: he crawled under. Upon so doing he was again confronted with a shock that would have caused a heart attack in any weaker ant. The world was immensely larger than he had dreamed. For it seemed that the anthill had been located under a bushel basket and what he thought was the outside world was only the area covered by the basket. But now he was faced with the whole world. He realized that he really had been unable to understand his environment until he had gotten out of it. Only now did he see that the anthill was covered by a bushel basket.

He still had not found his grasshopper, so he continued on. Again a barrier stopped him until he was able to burrow under it. And another shock greeted him. For once on the other side of the barrier he realized that the bushel basket was located in a greenhouse and that what he had thought was the big wide world was really only a small greenhouse. Now that he was outside the greenhouse he could understand.

Well, the story goes on because it turns out that the ant, intelligent as he might be, still didn't know where he was. For the greenhouse was located just outside center field of the Astrodome in Houston. And, you see, that ant really isn't any different from you or me.[9]

Debrief. Ask the students what the story tells them about their own place in the world. Ask them to consider the following questions: How significant are you? How small are you? How important was the ant? How important are you to yourself? How important did the ant feel?

---

[9]From *Teaching Human Beings: 101 Subversive Activities for the Classroom*. Copyright © 1972 by Jeffrey Shrank. Reprinted by permission of Beacon Press.

12 Social Service

164 SOCIAL MOVEMENTS

The protest movements of the '60s radically changed into a multitude of diverse objectives in the '70s. The folksinging, peaceful rebellion of 1963 graduated into bomb throwing, building burning by 1970. These minor violent groups quickly dissolved into self-improvement, self-discovery, return-to-the-earth movements during the '70s. Soon people were more concerned with maintaining their own environment than with changing the world. Thus people began to make their own clothes, bake their own bread, and cook with natural foods. Similarly they began to look inward and tried to find out what was going on in their heads. All over the country new types of consciousness-raising groups were being formed. Near most college campuses could be found encounter groups, Tarot card readers, astrologists, EST trainers, massage workshops, natural food stores, martial arts classes, acupuncture practitioners.

Have students identify some of these sources of self-improvement, self-discovery in their community. Ask some of these people to come in and talk about their lives and values. Have students develop a local directory of alternative lifestyles and alternative-value groups.

165 THE CRAFT REVIVAL

Have students identify all the craftspeople in their area and determine where they can purchase macrame work, ceramics, stained glass, natural food, natural wood products, homemade clothing, jewelry. Determine when the stores and craft-sale areas got started, and why, and discuss the backgrounds of the craftspeople who operate the alternative businesses.

Invite local craftspeople and self-discovery people to the classroom to teach their skills to the students or to lead discussions about their lifestyle.

166   HOW TO GET INVOLVED IN BETTERING
YOUR COMMUNITY

Below is a list of suggestions for ways in which your students may become overtly involved in the social issues of your community. Pass out this list, and have students develop additional ideas. Ask students to choose a project or projects to work on and to make journal entries regarding their work. Work will be evaluated on hours worked and results achieved. If students are not already keeping a journal, have them keep a journal of their experiences during this strategy.

1. Write to ACTION and find out what types of programs exist for you to get involved in.

2. Join a political organization such as the League of Women Voters, the Democratic Club, the Young Republicans.

3. Join an environmental organization such as the Sierra Club, the Costeau Society, or the Audubon Society, and become involved in some activity suggested in the organization's newsletter—a letter campaign around some environmental issue, a wilderness clean-up party, or the like.

4. Write a letter protesting the treatment of animals such as the killing of whales, timber wolves, baby seals, and others.

5. Donate your blood. Better yet, work with the Red Cross on having a blood-donation day at your school for those old enough to donate.

6. Join a political candidate's volunteer team, and work for his or her organization. Anything from stuffing envelopes to canvassing is a good learning experience.

7. Do some evaluative reporting to your city or county. Ride your mass-transit system extensively and evaluate it, or examine the local health care services, or study your educational system or your garbage disposal system or your juvenile justice system. Do some comparison study with other cities in your area.

8. Get involved in a voter-registration drive. Start by registering all the eighteen-year-olds in your own school.

9. Organize a committee of students to work with the school board on improvement of your school. Work toward getting a nonvoting student on the board as a member. Get all the high schools in your area to organize for common goals.

10. Organize a student committee that will advise your city council on problems facing youth.

11. Set up a tutoring program in which high school students would go to the junior high and grade schools to tutor.

12. Organize all the students in your state, and hire a lobbyist to go to the state capital to represent your views.

13. Establish a recycling center; not only will you clean up the city, but you will make some money that could be used for environmental education.

14. Lobby against junk food being sold on campus and in the cafeteria. Do a nutritional evaluation of the school's meals.

15. Do a teacher evaluation, and publish your report.

16. Volunteer your time to the recreation center, suicide-prevention center, VD clinic, or elsewhere.

17. Establish alternative/free/open/innovative courses in your school.

18. Get the local media to donate space or time regularly for news about and by students.

19. "Adopt" a child in another nation via a charitable organization or promote your town or city becoming a sister-community to one in another country.

20. Identify resource people in your community—lawyers, grant writers, teachers, psychologists, and so on—and get them to join your projects.

21. Establish a Youth Employment Service at your school.

22. Write letters to editors about causes that concern you.

23. Arrange for credit to be given for involvement in any of the activities listed in this strategy or devised by members of your class.

24. Find out about funding, and obtain funding for a project.

25. Get involved!

167   FORTY WAYS TO DEPOLLUTE THE EARTH

Have students brainstorm a list of ways that they can easily "depollute the earth," by lessening their demand on the earth's resources. The list might include simple things: place a brick in the toilet water tank; recycle hangers by taking your clothes to the cleaners on hangers; stop using dyed toilet and facial tissue; use less water through different techniques; turn the air conditioner thermostat up or the heater down; walk to the store rather than taking the car.

Each item on the list should suggest (1) an action that will help make the earth more environmentally sound and (2) a simple task that can be done with relatively small effort and expense.

Ask students to use the list as a plan of action at home. Ask them to attempt to accomplish as many of the items as they can during a one-month period, and give a report on their success at the end of the month.

Environmental groups are more than willing to contribute their suggestions for living an environmentally responsible life. The Sierra Club, the Cousteau Society, Greenpeace, the American Friends' Service Committee, and similar organizations should be contacted for materials.

Debrief. Was it easy for students to make such changes in their homes? Did their parents cooperate? Did students realize the extent of their impact on the environment before they became involved in this strategy?

168   LOCAL GUIDE TO SOCIAL SERVICES

Examine the list that follows to see if each item represents a need or problem experienced by people in your locale, and also if the service implied by each item is available in some form. Modify the list as necessary, but err on the side of retaining items rather than eliminating them. One goal of the strategy is to make students aware of how many people actually need and seek help of these kinds in nearly every community.

1. How to get help in a hospital emergency room
2. How to enroll a student (a little brother or sister) in grade school
3. How to find a child-care center
4. How to obtain legal services

5. How to get food stamps
6. How to apply for welfare assistance
7. How to get a job from an employment service
8. How to interview for a job if you are a stutterer
9. How to obtain medical care
10. How to locate your father quickly if he's in the military service and serving in a distant post.
11. How to find an apartment
12. How to apply for college entrance
13. How to apply for financial aid for college study
14. How to determine what social security benefits are available to you
15. How to evaluate the program of vocational school
16. Where to find psychological counseling services
17. What to do if you are worried about suicide
18. What to do if you have a drug problem
19. Your parents have just been killed—how do you get your brothers and sisters to relatives?
20. Your parents have just been killed—how would you arrange for their burial?
21. You aren't happy living at home. What other alternatives do you have?
22. You are new in town. What recreational facilities and programs are available to you?
23. What to do if you think you've been discriminated against
24. What to do if you think you have venereal disease

Then divide the class into two-person teams and ask each team to select a problem from the list.

One member of the team is to play the role of someone who has the problem or the need chosen. Ask these students to role play the situations as realistically as possible without placing a burden on the social agencies. They should live out the experiences. (The degree of possible realism will obviously vary; some students may be able to present themselves as bona fide clients of an agency, others may have to ask the personnel they encounter "What would happen if I _____? What would you do? What would I have to do?)

The other student is an observer/recorder, who makes the most complete on-the-spot and recall report of situations encountered as he or she can. It's often helpful for the observer/recorder to debrief with the role-player immediately after each situation.

After each team has identified the sources of help available to solve their problems and has gone through the process of solving the problems as far as possible, ask them to share their experiences with the whole class.

The class then should go on to research all available community social services that could affect youth and to write a guide to their locations, services, and procedures. Rate the agencies as to their responsiveness. Include in your catalog each agency's phone number, address and the name of a responsive person to contact if one has been identified.

Obtain a grant from a social agency to get the guide published and distributed.

Historical Methodology

This unit was developed to help teachers deal with perennial questions such as: "Why do I have to study history?" "Don't you think history is boring?" "What does history have to do with today's world?" "What does history have to do with me?"

The strategies in this unit will demonstrate to students that they are in fact very much interested in history, even if they have been turned off by history courses. The strategies in Section 1 will "hook" the students' interest. Once their interests and desires have been determined, you must provide the follow-up by gearing your course to meet the students' needs.

This unit attempts to get the students to function as historians rather than to become historical scholars. Section 2 introduces skills that allow the student to think and research like a historian. Section 3 allows the student to act like a historian. Section 4 presents some specific case studies that allow students to apply their skills.

The unit examines what history is and isn't and the problems involved in recording history. Techniques of discussion, simulation, role playing, case study, research, and problem solving are emphasized.

1 Developing Interest

169 ARE YOU INTERESTED IN HISTORY?

Have students write down the names of five people, living or dead, whom they would most like to talk to for an hour. List all their responses on the board in two *unlabeled* lists (one of living people and one of those now dead). Ask the group to tell you the difference between the two lists. (The list of people now dead is usually much longer than the list of people who are still alive.) Point out that the list of those now dead indicates an interest in history. Ask them to verbalize what types of questions they would like to ask those people if they could. Then suggest that your history course answer those questions.

170 FOUNDING FATHERS

Ask the students to decide whether the Founding Fathers, if they were to return to life today, would be happy or unhappy with how the country is being run and how the Constitution is being interpreted, and to discuss the reasons for their decisions.

171 HISTORICAL ROLE PLAYING

Ask five or six volunteers to each select a famous person in history—one whose attitudes and philosophies are known to them. The students are to assume that they are in heaven looking down on how the earth is being run now. They are to discuss what they see from the viewpoints of the people whose roles they are assuming.

Debrief. Did the students interject their own attitudes, or did they remain faithful to the point of view of the historical figure? Did they discover or wonder about aspects of the historical figure's views they hadn't considered before?

2 Acquiring Skills

172 DID HISTORY GET LOST IN TRANSLATION?

List the following characters on the board: Meriwether Lewis; William Clark; Sacajawea; Sacajawea's husband; the Mandan chief; Lewis and Clark's lieutenant. Have students volunteer to role play each role as Lewis and Clark seek directions and ask for help in crossing the mountains to reach the ocean.

After ten or fifteen minutes of role playing, stop the players, and ask the class to evaluate how realistic their portrayal was. List some of the responses of class members. They may mention, for instance, that the clothing was unrealistic, that the players' knowledge of the times was poor, that the place was not the same, that the language spoken was different. Press them about what language was spoken, and discuss the actual line of communication, which was: The Mandan chief (Mandan) could speak to Sacajawea (Shoshone) who could speak to her husband (French) who could speak to Lewis and Clark's lieutenant (French-English) who could speak to Lewis and Clark.

Debrief. How much of the chief's original idea probably was transmitted to Lewis and Clark? What does this exercise reveal to you about the accuracy of 3,000 years of *recorded* history?

173 BOTTICELLI, OR WHO AM I?

This strategy can be done in three different ways, based upon the historical knowledge of the group that is involved. The basic strategy is to send someone out of the room to decide which historical figure he or she will represent. The student then returns to the room and carries on a conversation with the class. The conversation is to be general, though leading in nature. Based upon the conversation, during which the group will try to narrow down the time period, era, geographical area, field of involvement, sex, and so on, someone will guess who the student is. Whoever guesses correctly may then select a historical figure to portray.

An alternative approach is for one person to leave the room while the class decides who that person will represent. The student returns and tries through the use of leading statements and questions to narrow down the time period, era, geographic area, field of involvement, sex, and so on of the person he or she represents in order to determine that person's identity. You may wish to volunteer to leave the room first; be willing to risk making yourself look a little silly (human).

Perhaps the simplest variation is to ask a volunteer to choose a famous person and to tell the class the first letter of that person's last name. A student asks questions that will narrow the field, the sex, the age, whether the person is living or dead, and so on, until the person gets a "no" answer; then the next person begins questioning. The person asking the questions can make a guess at any time. If the guess is wrong, the next questioner begins. The student who guesses correctly then assumes the role of a figure of his or her choice.

174   HOW DO YOU KNOW?

Pick a topic—the Taj Mahal, the landing on the moon, or anything at all—and ask the class if it really exists or if it actually occurred. As they discuss the question, give them no response except "How do you know?" After about forty minutes of frustration, lead the class into a discussion of what a historical fact is. What is historical research? Who does it? What is biased history? What does faith have to do with historical facts? Is everything printed in books true?

Next, examine two books on the same subject—the American Revolution as explained in an American textbook and an English textbook provides a great example. Discuss how the authors treat the same subject differently. Is one accurate and one inaccurate? How should history be read?

175   LIBRARY SEARCH AND SEIZURE

This strategy is to be completed in the research section of the most complete library in your locale, after a classroom discussion of the various types of reference sources available. The strategy will introduce students to the library layout and to a large number of reference books and library resources. The next time they visit the library on their own, they will be less overwhelmed and confused.

You may wish to visit the library as a group and join in a tour, or ask a reference librarian to point out the various reference books discussed in class, or lead such a tour yourself.

Distribute a list of questions to the students with these directions:

Where the question calls for some information, also include the source of the answer, using a full notation. You may seek the assistance of the librarian, but *only* the assistance. The librarian is not to do the assignment for you; he or she is much too busy for that. Explore the library yourself — it contains the answers to all your questions.

1. How did the *New Republic* review George Frost Kennan's book, *Memoirs 1925–50?*

2. How many magazine articles were written on War: Causes, from July, 1939, to June, 1941?

3. Ralph Andrist, a contemporary author, was born the son of a _____, and Andrist's politics are _____

4. According to the four editions of _____, the men's overall water ski champion in 1958 was _____

5. The *clear purpose* of the *Westminster Dictionary of Church History* is to: _____
   _____.

6. The best source of articles on education is: _____
   _____.

7. Minneapolis has _____ firms that furnish abdominal supports.

8. K. Ross Toole, University of Montana history professor, wrote his master's thesis on Marcus Daly — the thesis is now on the shelves as part of the _____ Collection. His thesis was written in the year _____ (Substitute information about a thesis to be found in the library you select.)

9. The first substantive line of Franklin D. Roosevelt's First Annual Message to Congress, delivered on January 3, 1934, was: _____
   _____.

10. According to the first line of John Foster Dulles's speech of June 10, 1954, was he inspired or uninspired?

11. If you look in the book with call number _____ (add a call number appropriate to the library you select), what would you find? Would you need to look at the book to find out?

12. Books on homosexuality have call numbers between _____ and

_____

13. If you wanted to know what paperback books were in print in 1974, you would look in: _____

14. How would you find out if a bibliography already exists on a subject you are researching?

15. How would you find out what the Puritans used for toilet paper?

    Obviously the point of these questions is not what the answers are but how and where the students find them.

3 Functioning as a Historian

176 HISTORY DISCUSSION QUESTIONS

Lead a discussion based on the following questions:

Why do people with amnesia hunt for their pasts? Why do some adoptees hunt for their background? What is the difference between current events and history? How does time effect history? (Documents are lost, emotionalism dies down, participants die, memoirs are written, documents are released.) Do people create history, or is it created by circumstances? by the times? Is it possible to write unbiased history? Do these two phrases—"nearly 1,000" and "less than 1,000"—mean the same thing? Does the choice of one over the other create a bias? Is there such a thing as *the* cause of history? What is history? (You may wish to refer to E. H. Carr's book of the same name.)

177 LOCAL HISTORY PROJECTS

Have students brainstorm a list of local history project topics, themes that they feel would be interesting ro research. Each student then chooses one for study. The student is not allowed to use books or journals to do research, and the student is not allowed to write a paper. The student must conduct interviews; go to museums; go to archives, special collections, newspaper morgues or library newspaper files, and company historical rooms and conduct on-site research and observation. The student then produces a brochure, tape recording, slide show, film, multi-media presentation, play, or other depiction on the research.

(A very successful project of this kind was done by Vickie Spencer, a junior. She involved her whole family in the retracing of the steps of Lewis and Clark through Montana. She used the journals of the explorers as her guide and took photographs of the most interesting areas they described. By using the journal descriptions and by going to the areas, she determined that a monument had been placed in the wrong spot to commemorate Lewis and Clark's overnight stay in her town. Three days after her class presentation, a University of Montana history professor published an article in the local paper stating the same conclusion. You can imagine the look on her face as she brought the newspaper article into class! She had revealed history, not studied it.)

178 HISTORY BY WINNERS

History is written by winners—those who won the wars and were thus able to write the history. But history loves losers. Do we remember that Napoleon lost or that Wellington won at Waterloo? Do we remember that Custer lost or that the Sioux, Cheyenne, and Blackfoot won at the Little Bighorn? Do we remember that Lee lost at Gettysburg, or do we remember Meade, who defeated him?

Have students examine their own textbook to see how losers are treated as compared to winners.

179 QUOTES FOR DISCUSSIONS OR TEST

Read the material in quotes and then discuss the italicized statements with the class. These quotes can also be used as a basis for an essay test.

Our knowledge of any past event is always incomplete, probably inaccurate, beclouded by ambivalent evidence and biased historians, and perhaps distorted by our own patriotic or religious partisanship. Most history is guessing and the rest is prejudice.[1] *[Therefore history is a waste.]*

Obviously historical methods cannot be a science. It can only be an industry of art, and a philosophy—an industry by ferreting out the facts, an art by establishing meaningful order in the chaos of materials, a philosophy by seeking perspective and enlightment.[2] *[Therefore historical methods are in need of constant evaluation and change.]*

[1]From *Historians' Fallacies* by David Hackett Fischer. Copyright © 1970 by David Hackett Fischer. Reprinted by permission of Harper & Row, Publishers, Inc.

[2]From *Lessons in History* by Will and Ariel Durant. Copyright © 1968 by Will and Ariel Durant. Reprinted by permission of Simon & Schuster.

American Culture

180 BUILDING NEW COMMUNITIES

This exercise can be used to introduce the study of the first Europeans who came to the New World and the eventual development of the nation and its Constitution. It can also be used as a futurism exercise.

First, discuss who was braver: Columbus, or the first men in space?

Read the introduction to *Shipwreck*. (The game is included in the Appendix, page 181.) Distribute copies of the fact sheet. Each day, read a problem to the class and let them discuss it until they have decided upon a solution that satisfies the group.

At the end of the seven problems (it generally takes longer than seven days to resolve them all), have the students read "The Twin Oaks Experiment" in *Psychology Today* (February, 1974) about the Twin Oaks commune. Have students do a comparison of Terra and Twin Oaks. They may also want to use William Golding's *Lord of the Flies,* or Henry David Thoreau's *Walden.*

Ask the students to consider these basic questions: How does what you learned by playing *Shipwreck* apply to the real world? What does the game tell you about your class and your place in the class? Would your society have been successful? Was your society patterned on socialism, capitalism, or communism? What was the philosophy of your society? How did those at Twin Oaks, or on the island in *Lord of the Flies,* or Thoreau at Walden solve some of the same problems? What does this exercise have to do with the colonial experience and the Constitutional Convention?

181 BODY RITUAL AMONG THE NACIREMA

After studying the techniques of anthropologists and archeologists, read your students the paper "The Body Ritual of the Nacirema" (included in the Appendix, pages 187–191). See if the students realize whom the paper is talking about. Discuss the techniques described in the paper.

Then have students select an object in the home—television, stereo, car, hair dryer, cigarettes, water bed, or some such—and make a cultural report on all the different aspects of the culture that left behind this one item. Have the students read the reports aloud.

182 100 PERCENT AMERICAN

To stimulate conversation about American culture, have students list items on the board that are 100 percent American and *part of the culture*. Remember that hamburgers and beer are German, Christmas is Scandanavian, ice cream is French, snowmobiles are Canadian, and so forth. This strategy will lead you to a discussion of the melting pot concept and the notion of ethnocentrism.

Finally, listen to the record "Mark Twain Tonight" by Hal Holbrook as an example of early American cultural humor.

Unit **V**

American Government: Three Simulations

The strategies in the final unit are much more complex than those in the earlier unit. This unit was written with juniors and seniors in mind; with minor adaptation, it could be geared to younger students.

The strategies emphasize the technique of simulation. Study some of the published simulation games that are recommended in the Appendix so that you have a model for developing your own simulations.

This unit is divided into three sections—one for each branch of government. The goal of each section is to have students experience—rather than study—how each branch of government functions. While simulation is the major technique used, the skills of research, problem solving, and decision making are also emphasized. Each strategy emphasizes verbal communication.

183 CRIME AND TRIAL: THE JUDICIAL BRANCH

After doing an academic study of the courts, introduce this strategy, which is even more involving than a trip to the courts. What could involve students more than to "commit" a crime and try the case in class?

Write a scenario for the crime. Involve as many characters as possible in order to give a large number of students a chance to participate. You might include defense attorneys, defense investigators, defense witnesses, prosecuting lawyers, prosecuting investigators, prosecution witnesses, members of the jury, press representatives, a bailiff, lab specialists, and criminals. Compile a list of characters and invite the students to select their roles. They are then assigned to do on-the-spot role research. The local federal judge, for example, may speak briefly from the bench to all the class witnesses and jurors while they sit in the jury box. The class defense attorneys may meet with representatives from the public defender's office, the prosecuting attorney may meet with the local district attorney; each person may be assigned someone in the community to give them on-the-spot experience. You may wish to contact a local law school to see whether two law students would assist each class lawyer's team in preparing their cases.

Once the scenario is written, type out on separate sheets of paper exactly what each criminal and witness is supposed to do and when, where, and how. Each person knows only what he or she will do; no one but the teacher knows the whole crime. (One of my instructions merely read: "Be at the corner of 8th and Market from 8:00 P.M. until 8:05 P.M., then go home." If the student observed anything, fine.)

Next you might wish to contact the juvenile authorities and tell them of your project. (The "criminals" in one of my classes were unaware of the fact that the police were to participate in the simulation; the officers were waiting for the "criminals," had them spread-eagle on the ground, handcuffed them, and put them in a cell. The "criminals" then had to call their "lawyers" to come get them out. Those students representing the press had been assigned to be at the jail at the time the students were to be brought in. One policeman purposely did not read the criminal his rights. The willingness of the police to participate was most helpful and made the whole case realistic.) The "criminals" leave physical evidence that the "lab people" must find and interpret. Next, the lawyers must determine who were witnesses and who was the jury. (Many witnesses didn't really know for days that they had witnessed anything.) The case is then tried in the classroom.

(Once the classroom trial started, the most highly paid attorney in town took two hours out on two different days to preside as the judge. He, too, made the situation realistic; the police came in to testify as well.)

After the jury makes a decision, spend a couple of days debriefing the whole experience. (The police and the judge helped greatly in this process.)

185 THE ELECTIVE PROCESS: THE EXECUTIVE BRANCH

After you have studied the American presidential campaign and election process, put this knowledge into operation. Because local school issues are less complex than national and international issues, it helps to use the school as a microcosm of national concepts. Students from one class period can compete against students from another. But you could also divide up one class into two parties or use more than two classes.

1. Have your students brainstorm a list of twenty "issues" at the school.

2. From this list, write a testing scale consisting of twenty policy or position statements. These should be written so that students can respond in terms of agreement—5 indicates *full agreement;* 1 indicates *absolute nonagreement.* Remember all statements must be written from the same slant—either all liberal or all conservative.

3. Read the questions, and have students give their responses to each on the scale of 1 to 5, then add up the score and divide by 20.

4. Next form a circle beginning with the highest score in descending order to the lowest.

5. Now divide the circle into six equal parts, using the scores as division points. Put more people in the first two groups if the number doesn't come out even. Two people make up a state, and three states make up a bloc. Each bloc should be given a name.

6. Each bloc must now work on three planks that they would like to see the party candidate run on.

7. Each bloc elects a representative to the Executive Platform Committee.

8. The Executive Platform Committee meets and elects a chairperson.

9. Of the eighteen proposed planks, the committee can pass only six—only committee members may speak, although diplomatic notes from outside may be passed to the committee by pages. The committee can also recess to lobby or meet with bloc members. Similar planks can be combined into one plank, with both blocs getting credit for passage. A majority vote—four blocs—is needed for passage.

10. After the six blocs have passed the executive platform, the individual states meet and name their delegates. Then assign delegate votes. The top-scoring state should have about 12 to 15 votes; the middle states, 7 to 11; the low states, 3 to 8. The top two states should clearly have more votes than any two middle states (coalition of California and New York over Oklahoma and Montana).

11. The individual states now work out three planks that are extremely important to them personally. These are then typed out; the state proposing the planks and an identification number are also listed.

12. The convention is then opened. The Executive Committee chairperson acts as chairperson of the convention.

13. The convention adopts an eighteen-plank agenda. The agenda will be considered in order. Each state has *one vote* to establish agenda.

14. Once the eighteen agenda items are established, the convention is open to discuss, debate, combine similar planks, and vote on the general platform. Voting on the platform is now done by delegate strength. Delegates may split their votes. A two-thirds majority is now needed to adopt an item. The convention can adopt only six planks. Thus the total platform will be twelve planks. Remember, use of parliamentary strategy is a must; lobbying and use of the recesses is most important. Also remember that your candidate must be able to run on your platform.

15. After the platform is adopted, a six-member Style and Syntax Committee is established by a 51-percent vote to rework the planks into a presentable platform for the candidate. The platform would include justification and arguments for the planks.

16. Next, the convention turns to the nomination of the presidential candidate. Candidates must have a nominating and a seconding speech. The vote is done by delegate votes, and to be nominated a candidate needs a two-thirds majority.

17. Once the candidate is chosen, his or her state delegate vote is then increased by 10.

18. The convention then elects candidates for vice-president, secretary, and treasurer. Remember, the candidates are running for school offices on school issues.

19. The presidential candidate is allowed to name his or her campaign manager and the heads of the various campaign committees.

20. The convention must now adopt the Style and Syntax Committee report by a majority vote.

21. Begin to campaign throughout the school.

22. Each campaign is given 10 million dollars to spend. Expenditures must be reported each day to the Election Watch Dog Committee. This committee makes all rulings on dirty tricks, and decides all punishments. It costs $100 for any sign, button, or paper worn on the body, $500 for any butcher-paper-sized banner, $500 for each ten-second spot on the school public address system, $1,000 for use of the video recorder for each ten seconds, $5,000 for each story in the school paper about the candidate, and $15,000 for each public appearance of the candidate. The charge for each public endorsement you get from other school class officers is $5,000; $10,000 is the cost of each public endorsement by a teacher; and $15,000 is the cost of a public endorsement by an administrator.

23. After the campaign, the school votes.

Points are awarded and grades assigned based upon the following schedule:

Number of
Points   *Point winners*

10	Member, Executive Committee
10	Chairperson, Executive Committee
5	Member, bloc of chairperson of Executive Committee
10	Member, bloc that sponsored passing plank (10 points per plank)
5	Member, state delegation that sponsored an item included on the agenda (5 points per item)
10	Member, state delegation that sponsored passing plank
10	Member, Style and Syntax Committee
20	Member, state delegation of presidential candidate

Number of
points   *Point winners*

15	Member, state delegation of vice-presidential candidate
10	Member, state delegation of candidate for secretary
10	Member, state delegation of candidate for treasurer

Number of points	Point winners
15	Member, state delegation of campaign manager
5	Member, state delegation of committee head appointee
25	Member, state delegation with winning candidate in final election
25	Each member of the party with a winning candidate
25	Member, party whose *whole state* won
10	Each winning individual

Debrief. Evaluate the simulation. People who are not happy with their grades may write debriefing papers.

185   LOBBYING: THE LEGISLATIVE BRANCH

Select any controversial subject—you may find it simplest to deal first with a school problem. Briefly state two extreme views of the question. If your topic is, for example, abortion, state the position of those who view abortion as appropriate in all cases in which it is requested, and also the position of those who believe that abortion is never appropriate. Then have students line up along the chalkboard according to how strongly they believe in one of the two positions. Those who agree completely with one position stand to the left, those who agree with the other stand to the right, and those who are undecided stand in the middle. For five minutes, allow the people at the extreme positions to lobby the middle people into lining up with them and to explain why they should move. At the end of the five minutes, have the students line up again, and see which students have changed their minds. Repeat the process with regard to four or five questions.

Debrief. How was the lobbying done? Which techniques were effective and which weren't? Discuss the positive and negative effects of lobbying in Washington.

Appendix

Sources of Affective Domain Tests

STRATEGY 5

California Test of Personality (self-reliance)

    California Test Bureau
    Del Monte Research Park
    Monterey, CA 93940

Edwards Personality Inventory (articulation; ability to assume responsibility; enjoyment of being center of attention; leadership; ability to make friends; shyness)

    Science Research Associates
    259 E. Erie Street
    Chicago, IL 60611

Measurement of Affect: The Humanizing of Education

    Interstate Educational Resource
      Service Center
    1610 University Club Building
    136 East South Temple
    Salt Lake City, UT 84111

Motivation for School Achievement
Journal of Educational Research,

1969, Vol. 62 (6), pp. 263-266.

Minnesota Counseling Inventory (leadership; adjustment to reality)

    Psychological Corporation
    304 West 45th Street
    New York, NY 10017

Purpose in Life Test

    Psychometric Affiliate
    1743 Monterey
    Chicago, IL 60643

Scales for the Measurement of Attitudes (acceptance of others and self)

    McGraw-Hill
    330 West 42nd Street
    New York, NY 10036

Self-Esteem Inventory

    Stanley Coopersmith
    3111 Brewster Court
    El Cerrito, CA 94530

Self-Perception Inventory (self-actualization)

    Martin Psychologists and Educators, Inc.
    211 West State Street, Suite 217
    Jacksonville, IL 62650

Sixteen Personality Factors Question-naire (Form A, Factor H; forthright-ness versus shrewdness)

   Institute for Personality and Abil-ity Testing
   1602 Coronada Drive
   Champaign, IL 61820

Social Insight Test

   Consulting Psychologist Press, Inc.
   577 College Avenue
   P.O. Box 11636
   Palo Alto, CA 94306

Specific Fear Index
Journal of Abnormal and Social Psy-chology,
1956, Vol. 52, pp. 171-178.

Tennessee Self-Concept Scale (coun-selor, recordings, and tests)

   Box 6184
   Acklen Station
   Nashville, TN 37212

Sample Test Packet

STRATEGY 74

Second Grader's Name: _____

Station 1   Coordinator: **Bill**
Grab Bag

Ask the children to identify grab-bag items by feeling them.

	Correct Guess	*Incorrect Guess*
Jaw breaker		
Sponge		
Leather bracelet		
Barette		
Seashell		
Yo-yo		
Toy gun		
Banana		

Taste (or Smell)	*Correct Guess*	*Incorrect Guess*

Ask the children to close their eyes, hold their noses, taste a number of items, and guess what they are.

Comments:

Station **2.** *Coordinator:* **Joan**

Personal Evaluation.

Ask the children the following questions. Record all responses, and indicate how the children reacted to the interview: Were they confident? nervous? Did they have a good command of the language?

1. How many brothers and sisters do you have?
2. What number are you in the family?
3. Do both your parents live in your home?
4. Do you like being in this school?
5. Who in the group do you like best, and why?
6. What do you want to be when you grow up?
7. What does your mother do?
8. What does your father do?
9. Do you like yourself?
10. Are you happy with the way you look? Why, or why not?
11. If you could change anything about yourself, what would you change?
12. If you could change anything in the world, what would you change?

Station **3.** *Coordinator:* **Julia**

Abstraction

Record the children's responses to the following questions, noting their reactions. Were they nervous? confident? shy? Did they have good command of the language? Did they display imagination? Were they able to think abstractly?

1. How long is forever?
2. Have children determine when a minute has elapsed; do the same for fifteen seconds.
3. What is time?

4. What do you dream about?

5. Why do you have five fingers?

6. What is love?

7. What could you buy with a penny? a dollar?

8. What do you watch on television?

9. Show children a picture, and have them explain what is occurring.

Station 4. Coordinator: **Jane**

Self-Portrait

Have the children feel their faces with their eyes closed and describe what they feel and whether or not they like it. Record all their responses. Then have each child draw a self-portrait.

Station 5. Coordinator: **Maureen**

Clay Play.

Observe a small group working with clay. What do they try to make? Who copies, and who takes the initiative? Record your observations below.

Station 6. Coordinator: **John**

Balance Beam.

Record the number of times students fall going down frontward and coming back backward. Record their reactions. Are they nervous? confident?

Throwing and Catching.

Record the number of times students catch ball or miss it, how far they can throw it, and how they react to this experiment.

Standing Balance.

Have students shut their eyes and stand on one foot. Do they fall? How confident are they?

Headstand.

Can they stand on their heads? How much coordination do they have? Are they afraid?

Coordination.

Ask students to hold their arms out to their sides, close their eyes and then try to bring their first fingers together tip to tip out in front of them. Can they do it?

Demonstrate the following physical activities to children, and then have them attempt to imitate each activity.

Copied Skills in Dance

Elephant Walk:

Twist:

Jumping Jacks:

Combination 1: (a sequence of two or three specific movements)

Combination 2:

Free Dance Interpretation

Describe in each area how the kids did, their confidence, how they reacted to the group, whether they were shy or inhibited, and any general things you observed that gave you an indication as to their personality and development.

Please Hear
What I Am Not Saying

Don't be fooled by me. Don't be fooled by the face I wear. I wear a mask, I wear a thousand masks, masks that I am afraid to take off, and none of them are me.

Pretending is an art that is second nature with me, but don't be fooled; for God's sake, don't be fooled. I give you the impression that I am secure, that all is sunny and unruffled within me as well as without; that confidence is my name and coolness my game; that the water is calm and I am in command; that I need no one. But don't believe me, please. . . . My surface may seem smooth, but my surface is my mask, my ever-varying and ever-concealing mask.

Beneath lies no smugness, no complacence. Beneath dwells the real me in confusion, in fear, in aloneness. But I hide this. I don't want anybody to know it. I panic at the thought of my weakness and fear of being exposed. That's why I frantically create a mask to hide behind; a nonchalant, sophisticated facade, to help me pretend, to shield me from the glance that knows. But such a glance is precisely my salvation. And I know it. That is, if it's followed by acceptance, if it's followed by LOVE.

It's the only thing that can liberate me from myself; from my own self-built prison walls; from the barriers I so painstakingly erect. It's the only thing that will assure me of what I can't assure myself, that I am really something.

But I don't tell you this; I don't dare. I'm afraid to. I'm afraid your glance will not be followed by acceptance and love. I'm afraid you'll think less of me, that you'll laugh, and your laugh would kill me; I'm afraid that deep down I'm nothing, that I'm just no good and that you will see this and reject me.

So I play my game, my desperate, pretending game, with a facade of assurance without and a trembling child within.

And so, begins the parade of masks, the glittering but empty parade of masks. My life becomes a front. I idly chatter to you in suave tones of surface talk. I tell you everything that is nothing and nothing that is everything, of what's crying inside me. So when I'm going through my routine, do not be fooled by what I am saying.

Please listen carefully and try to hear what I am not saying, *what I would like to be able to say,* what for survival I need to say, but what I can't say.

I dislike hiding, honestly. I dislike the superficial game I am playing, the superficial phony. I'd like to be really genuine and spontaneous and me, but you've got to help me. You've got to hold out your hand even when that's the last thing I seem to want or need. Only you can wipe away from my eyes the blank stare of the breathing dead. Only you can call me into *aliveness.* Each time you're kind and gentle and encouraging, each time you try to understand because you really care, my heart begins to grow wings, very small wings, very feeble wings, but wings.

With your sensitivity and compassion and your power of understanding, you can breathe life into me. I want you to know that, I want you to know how important you are to me. How you can be the creator of the person that is me if you choose to. PLEASE CHOOSE. You alone can break down the wall behind which I tremble; you alone can remove the mask; you alone can release me from my lonely prison. Do not pass me by. Please do not pass me by. It will not be easy for you. My long conviction of worthlessness builds strong walls. The nearer you approach me, the more blindly I might strike back. It's irrational, but despite what books say about a person, I am irrational. I fight against the very thing I cry out for.

But I am told that love is stronger than strong walls, and in this lies hope. MY ONLY HOPE. Please try to beat down my wall with firm hands, but with gentle hands—for a child is very sensitive. Who am I, you may wonder? I am someone you know very well. FOR I AM EVERY MAN YOU MEET. I AM EVERY WOMAN YOU MEET. I AM RIGHT IN FRONT OF YOU!

Divorce Course[1]

For years, thousands of U.S. high schools have taught "life adjust-ment" courses to introduce adolescents to the trials and tribulations of marriage. Since 1970, Parkrose High School in Portland, Oregon has been carrying the instruction one step further; its twelve-week course on contemporary family life starts with the students pretending to get married—and ends with them pretending to get divorced.

The Parkrose divorce course was designed by History Teacher Cliff Allen, a former football coach, as a "simulation game" to teach "the reality of marriage—no punches pulled." Allen, 35, who has been married for 16 years, makes the game as real as he can. The class of twelve boys and twelve girls spends the first week or so pairing off as "husbands" and "wives." A computer matches their interests and personality traits; an anonymous student committee makes the final pairings.

Allen holds mock weddings complete with flowers, plastic wed-ding rings, organ music, and receptions. Most of the weddings are in the classroom, but last spring one couple decided to get married under the cherry trees on the school's front lawn. Some 300 students at-tended the ceremony.

The weddings are only the beginning. The couples must search for an apartment and sign a mock lease, read want ads and go through the motions of getting a job (they must persuade an employer to write a note guaranteeing one of them a job at a specified salary). They also prepare a budget and have a baby (simulated by the showing of a movie of a live birth). Later in the course, after they have been "mar-ried" for five years, the couples study real estate ads, get a multiple listing book, choose a house, and shop for furniture. "They just don't know what things cost."

The classes are enlivened by guest appearances—an insurance agent, realtor, clergyman, marriage counselor, and banker. But the

---

[1]*Time*, December 2, 1974. Reprinted by permission from *Time*, The Weekly Newsmaga-zine; Copyright Time, Inc., 1974.

students sometimes have firsthand experiences of their own. During one lecture on abortions, an 18-year-old girl rose to announce that she had had three abortions herself. She was invited to take over the discussion. The final outside expert is a lawyer who explains how to file for divorce. Last year, as an added touch of realism, Allen brought in a recent—and embittered—divorcee to talk about financial problems. "She really gave the kids a jolt," he says. Toward the end of the course, the couple must spin a "wheel of misfortune" that lists nine possible catastrophes (for example, the breadwinner is fired, the mother-in-law moves in or part of the house burns), all of which lead eventually to divorce.

Contemporary Family Life is an extremely popular course; 360 of Parkrose's class of 450 seniors have signed up for it, and there is a waiting list. About 600 other high schools have written for Allen's 60-page course outline, and the state departments of education in Utah and California have expressed interest in including the course in statewide high school curriculums.

Despite sometimes disillusioning insights that they received, about 50 couples who were paired in the course during the past four years have since been married. Allen says he does not know if any of them have been divorced.

A School Critique[2]

STRATEGY 120

1. A school is good when its daily time sequences are not arbitrary (45 minutes for this, 45 minutes for that, and so on) but are related to what the students are doing.

2. A school is good when students are not expected to do the same thing in the same amount of time.

3. A school is good when students are not required merely to serve time in courses, as in a jail sentence. Thus in a good school the question is not "have you taken . . . ?" but "have you learned . . . ?"

4. A school is good when it allows students, at least to some extent, to organize their own time.

5. A school is good when the activities it requires are not arbitrary (for example, "We've always done that") or based on discredited claims (for example, "The study of grammar strengthens the mind").

6. A school is good when it can assert on some empirical and rational basis that its activities have relevance to the lives of students.

7. A school is good when it does not require all students to engage in the same activities but gives them considerable latitude in choosing from among many options.

8. A school is good when it recognizes that no matter how logical its activity structuring may be, the process is next to worthless if students are alienated from the activities.

---

[2]Adapted from *The School Book* by Neil Postman and Charles Weingartner. Copyright © 1973 by Neil Postman and Charles Weingartner. Used by permission of the publisher, Delacorte Press.

157

9. A school is good when its activities are student activities. Student work should have some relationship to what scholars in a particular field actually do.

10. A school is good when its activities are not confined to a single building but include the resources of the whole community.

11. A school is good when its activities bring together students with great diversity of background and ability.

12. A school is good when it moves away from valuing memorization and ventriloquizing and moves toward valuing questioning, problem solving, and research.

13. A school is good when it rejects passive acceptance and encourages involvement and independence.

14. A school is good when it moves away from valuing knowledge "for knowledge's sake" and moves toward valuing the use of knowledge in daily life.

15. A school is good when reading ability is considered only one of several possible ways through which students can express intellectual competence and interest.

16. A school is good when it accepts as legitimate many of the new subjects invented, say, during the past 75 years or so—for example, anthropology, sociology, cinematography, ecology, cybernetics, linguistics, meteorology, marine biology, musicology, futuristics, urbanology, and others.

17. A school is good when it includes, as part of its definition of worthwhile knowledge, self-knowledge—that is, knowledge of what is going on inside one's skin.

18. A school is good when it moves away from aversive responses and toward reinforcing ones. By eliminating the stigma of failure, you eliminate a great deal of fear and anxiety, neither of which contributes to enthusiastic learning.

19. A school is good when it moves away from the factorylike processing procedures and toward more humanistic, individualized judgments. The idea is to make evaluation a learning experience, which, in theory, all schools recommend but which, in practice, few accomplish.

20. A school is good when its priorities are broadly conceived, rather than narrowly hierarchical. For example, in many schools a stu-

dent may be judged slow solely on the basis of reading and mathematical ability. The same student may be an excellent musician, actor, or even group leader but will receive very little formal recognition for these skills.

21. A school is good when it makes as explicit as possible the kinds of behavior it wants to encourage, assuming that such behaviors are reasonable.

22. A school is good when it does not use standardized tests, or uses them only with extreme caution and skepticism.

23. A school is good when it makes use of constructive, nonpunitive procedures for the evaluation of teachers and administrators, as well as students.

24. A school is good when it moves away from adversary relationships between teacher and student and toward collaborative effort.

25. A school is good when students are given opportunities to supervise themselves.

26. A school is good when it is small enough that supervision (and just about everything else) can be a personal—that is, human—problem, not a logistics problem.

27. A school is good when teachers forego their role as authority figures alone, view themselves as learners, and try to develop the idea of a learning community in which the teacher functions more as a coordinator or facilitator of activities than as a dictator.

28. A school is good when it places in a teaching role the greatest variety of people—for example, paraprofessionals, interested laypeople, and even students.

29. A school is good when it is so organized that it can capitalize on what its teachers do best and know most about.

30. A school is good when students are not objects to which things happen but are encouraged to be active shapers of their own school experiences.

31. A school is good when students are not constantly placed in competitive roles with each other but function instead in collaborative relationships.

32. A school is good when it moves away from bureaucratic paternalism and toward increased community participation.

33. A school is good when it offers a variety of alternative programs to the many publics that comprise a community.

34. A school is good when it is not afraid to be held accountable for its performance.

35. A school is good when its concept of knowledge, attitudes, and skills are oriented toward the future.

36. A school is good when it interprets its responsibility to the future as a responsibility to its students first, and to other social institutions (for example, colleges, businesses, the professions) only at a late and convenient hour.

Wad-Ja-Get?[3]

STRATEGY 121

Our grading system should:

1. Eliminate the anxiety which usually goes with grading.
2. Create a relaxed learning atmosphere in the class.
3. Decrease competition for grades among students.
4. Be meaningful—that is, a student's grades should mean something to him or her, personally.
5. Respect quality of work, as well as quantity.
6. Allow those students who needed a high grade to get one.

Is this your grading system?

1. We believe grades have become more important to students than learning.
2. Grades encourage cheating.
3. Grades divide teachers and students into warring camps.
4. Grades discourage students from developing their own goals.
5. Grading stifles creativity.
6. Grades are not applied fairly.
7. Grades create an unhealthy atmosphere in the school.
8. Grades support the other problems in school.

Did you know many teachers take these factors into consideration when giving grades?

1. student's IQ
2. final exams at the end of the semester
3. effort on part of student

---

[3]From *Wad-Ja-Get? The Grading Game in American Education* by Howard Kirschenbaum, Rodney W. Napier, and Sidney B. Simon, copyright 1971, Hart Publishing Company, Inc.

4. student's popularity
5. class participation
6. student's social class
7. student's ability to tell teachers what they want to hear
8. whether a student argues with the teacher or not
9. grading on the curve

Do these equations make sense to you?

History + Research + Experience = Arguments against Traditional Grades
Teacher Ease + Administrative Convenience + College Admissions Procedures = Forces That Maintain Traditional Grades

Alternative methods:

1. Written evaluation: Teacher merely explains what the student has accomplished and where the student needs improvement.

2. Self-evaluation: Student writes up an evaluation, as above, then assigns a grade to the work accomplished.

3. Give grades, but don't tell the students: Transcripts are kept and sent to colleges, but students never know their grades—thus stopping peer competition.

4. Contract system: Student writes a contract stating exactly what work is to be done at what level of mastery in exchange for what grade; when the contract is fulfilled the grade is assigned.

5. Mastery approach: Student continues to do the exercises until he or she achieves a 90-percent performance, then moves to next exercise.

6. Pass/fail: Student receives either a passing grade or a failing mark; there is no in-between.

7. Credit/no credit: If the student completes the work at a satisfactory level, a credit is assigned; if not, the student receives no credit (no credit is *not* the same as a fail).

8. Blanket grading: Every student in the class is given the same grade.

Indian Paradox

The United Native Americans (UNA) is proud to announce that it has bought the State of Montana from the Whites and is throwing it open to American Indian settlement. UNA bought Montana from three winos found wandering in Glendive. The winos promptly signed the treaty, which was written in the Northern Cheyenne language, and sold Montana for three bottles of wine, one bottle of gin, and four cases of beer.

The Honorable Richard E. Little Bear, the new commissioner of Caucasian Affairs, has announced the following new policies:

The Indians hereby generously give the Whites four enormously huge reservations of ten acres each at the following locations: In the middle of Makoshika Park, in the Badlands of South Dakota, in the Utah Salt Flats, and in the Yukon. These reservations shall belong to the whites for as long as the sun shines and the grass grows, or until such time as the Indians want them back.

All land on the reservations, of course, will be held in trust for the Whites by the Bureau of Caucasian Affairs, and any White who wants to use his land in any way must secure the permission of Commissioner Little Bear.

Of course, Whites will be allowed to sell or trade handicrafts at stands by the highway. Each White will be provided annually with one blanket and one pair of tennis shoes, a supply of Spam, and a copy of *My Life among the White People*. The latter was written as an exposé by a former Indian student at an all-White high school.

If any American Indian proves incompetent enough, he may qualify to be superintendent at any of the four above-mentioned Bureau of Caucasian Affairs' reservations that have been so generously set aside by the United Native Americans. Applicants for the superintendents' jobs must have less than a year of education, must not be able to understand Caucasian languages or customs, must have an authoritarian personality, must have proof of dishonesty, and must have a certificate of incompetence. Of course no Whites need apply.

Commissioner Little Bear also announced the founding of four boarding schools to which white youngsters will be sent at the age of six. "We want to take those white kids far away from the backward culture of their parents," the Commissioner said. The schools will be located on Alcatraz Island, in the Florida Everglades, at Point Barrow, Alaska, and at nearby Hong Kong.

All of their courses will be taught in the Indian languages, and demerits will be given to anyone caught speaking English. All students arriving at the school will immediately be given IQ tests to determine their understanding of Indian languages and hunting skills.

Hospitals will be established for the reservations in the following places: the Whites at Utah Salt Flats Caucasian Reservation may go to the Bangor, Maine, hospital; those at the South Dakota Badlands may go to the Juneau, Alaska, hospital; those at the Yukon may go to the hospital in Miami Beach, Florida; and those at the Makoshika Reservation can just forget it. Each Hospital will have a staff of two part-time doctors and a part-time chiropractor who have all passed, at least, first-aid tests; each hospital will be equipped with a scapel, a jack-knife, a saw, a modern tourniquet, and a large bottle of aspirin.

In honor of the Whites, many cities, streets, cars, and products will be given traditional Caucasian names. One famous Indian movie director has even announced that in his upcoming film, *Custer's Last Stand,* he will use many actual Whites to play the parts of the soldiers, speaking real English, although, of course, the part of Custer will be played by Tonto.

Certain barbaric white customs will not be allowed. Whites will not be permitted to practice their heathen religions and will be required to attend Indian ceremonies. Missionaries will be sent from each tribe to convert the Caucasians of the reservations. White churches will either be made into amusement parks or museums or will be torn down and the bricks and ornaments sold as souvenirs and curiosities.

The Chitterling Test[4]

STRATEGY 132

1. "T-Bone Walker" got famous for playing what?
   a. trombone
   b. piano
   c. "T-flute"
   d. guitar
   e. "ham bone"
2. A "gas head" is a person who has a
   a. fast-moving car.
   b. stable of "lace."
   c. "process."
   d. habit of stealing cars.
   e. long jail record for arson.
3. If a man is called a "blood," then he is a
   a. fighter.
   b. Mexican American.
   c. Afro-American.
   d. Redman, or Indian.
   e. hungry hemophile.
4. If you throw dice and "7" is showing on top, what is facing down?
   a. seven
   b. snake eyes
   c. box cars
   d. Little Joe
   e. eleven
5. Jazz pianist Ahmad Jamal took an Arabic name after becoming famous. Previously he had some fame with what he called his "slave name." What was his previous name?
   a. Willie Lee Jackson
   b. LeRoi Jones

---

[4]By Adrian Dove

165

    c. Wilbur McDougal
    d. Fritz Jones
    e. Andy Johnson

6. Cheap "chitlings" (not the kind you buy frozen at the frozen food counters) will taste rubbery unless they are cooked long enough. How soon can you quit cooking them to eat and enjoy them?
    a. fifteen minutes
    b. two hours
    c. twenty-four hours
    d. one week on a low flame
    e. one hour

7. A "hype" is a person who
    a. always says he feels sick.
    b. has water on the brain.
    c. uses heroin.
    d. is always ripping and running.
    e. is always sick.

8. What is Willie Mae's last name?
    a. Schwartz
    b. Matauda
    c. Gomez
    d. Turner
    e. O'Flaherty

9. The opposite of square is
    a. round.
    b. up.
    c. down.
    d. hip.
    e. lame.

10. "Money don't get everything, it's true,
    a. but I don't have none and I'm so blue."
    b. but what it don't get I can't use."
    c. so make do with what you've got."
    d. but I don't know that and neither do you."

11. A "hankerchief head" is
    a. a cool cat.
    b. a porter.
    c. an Uncle Tom.
    d. a hoddi.
    e. a preacher.

12. Which word is out of place here?
    a. Splib
    b. Blood

    c. Grey

    d. Spook

    e. Black

13. If a pimp is uptight with a woman who gets state aid, what does it mean when he talks about Mother's Day?

    a. second Sunday in May

    b. third Sunday in June

    c. first of every month

    d. first and fifteenth of every month

14. What are the Dixie Hummingbirds?

    a. a part of the KKK

    b. a swamp disease

    c. a modern gospel group

    d. a Mississippi Negro paramilitary striking force

    e. deacons

15. Bo-Diddley is a

    a. camp for children.

    b. cheap wine.

    c. singer.

    d. new dance.

    e. Mojo call.

16. *Jet* is

    a. an East Oakland motorcycle.

    b. one of the gangs is *West Side Story*.

    c. a news and gossip magazine.

    d. a way of life for the rich set.

17. Tell it _____ it is, baby.

    a. as

    b. how

    c. like

18. In the term "C. C. Rider," what does "C. C." stand for?

    a. civil service

    b. church council

    c. country circuit preacher

19. "Bird" or "Yardbird" was the "jacket" that his jazz admirers hung on

    a. Lester Young.

    b. Benny Goodman.

    c. Charlie Parker.

    d. the Birdman of Alcatraz.

20. "You've got to get up early in the morning to

    a. catch worms."

    b. be healthy, wealthy, and wise."

c. fool me."
d. be the first one on the street."
21. People say "Juneteenth" (June 10) should be a legal holiday because this was the day when
   a. Lincoln freed the slaves.
   b. Texas freed its slaves.
   c. Martin Luther King was born.
   d. Booker T. Washington died.
22. "Down-home" (in the South) today, for the average "soul brother" who is picking cotton from sunup til sundown, what is the average earning (take home) for one full day?
   a. $.75   b. $1.65   c. $3.50   d. $5.00   e. $12.00
23. "Hully Gully" came from
   a. East Oakland.
   b. Fillmore.
   c. Watts.
   d. Harlem.
   e. Motor City.

Answers:

1. d	9. d	17. c
2. c	10. b	18. c
3. c	11. c	19. c
4. a	12. c	20. d
5. d	13. c	21. c
6. c	14. c	22. d
7. c	15. c	23. c
8. d	16. c	

Hidden Persuaders[5]

[5]Copyright 1957 by Vance Packard. Adapted from the book *The Hidden Persuaders*, published by David McKay Co., Inc. Reprinted by permission of the publisher.

STRATEGY 140

Detergents

Women were given three different-colored boxes—blue, yellow, and blue/yellow—containing the same detergent. After testing the detergent in each box, the women reported that the detergent in the blue box left their clothes dirty and that the detergent in the yellow box was too strong. The detergent in the blue/yellow box won overwhelmingly favorable comments.

Toothpaste

Research studies showed that people do not brush their teeth to get particles out of their teeth and thus fight decay. In fact, they do it to get clean breath and a clean-mouth feeling.

Whisky

Of the amount of whisky sold, 65 percent is drunk by 22 percent of the drinkers. A man would not drink unless drinking changed his personality enough to satisfy him.

Gasoline

People were asked to draw cars—from the drawings, a psychologist could tell what kind of gasoline they would buy. The type of gasoline you purchase reveals the type of person you are. Long, streamlined cars usually were drawn by local successes or people whose yearnings for success were frustrated. They would buy the gasoline advertised around the theme of power and bigness. Cars drawn in a grand style but with detail indicated that gas would be purchased from the company that professed to be friendly and the neighborhood-type station—these people would like to get out of their cars and chat with the attendants. The artist who drew a flamboyant car that was not likely to run but had a lot of gadgets saw the car as a plaything; that person would buy the gasoline that promised to give you more fun going.

Cars

People were asked to associate a personality type with a certain car. *Cadillac*—proud, flashy, a salesman, middle-aged, socially mobile, good income, responsible; *Ford*—speed demon, good income, young man, proud, upper-class, drives to work, practical; *Pontiac*—stable, middle of the road, married woman, mother, sincere, conventional, busy; *Studebaker*—neat, sophisticated, intellectual, mobile, professional, young man.

Men are more attracted to convertibles but buy sedans; they associate convertibles with a mistress. The hardtop was a boon to sales; it promised the best of both worlds. Salesroom windows usually display a convertible in order to get the man inside.

Cigarettes

Although 65 percent of smokers are absolutely loyal to their brand and 20 percent are relatively loyal, in tests they can't tell the difference in brands.

A psychologist tested a group of cigarette smokers with personality tests. He then stated with only a few errors which brand of cigarettes each would smoke. Why do people smoke despite the warnings? (To relieve tension, to express sociability, as a reward for effort, as an aid to poise, as an aid in anticipating stress, as proof of daring, as proof of conformity, because it is an accustomed ritual.) Americans smoke to prove they are virile, vigorous, potent.

Cigars

The cigar is the biggest symbol of potency available for a dime. Associated with masculine toughness—gangsters, bank presidents. Big men, and men who want to be big smoke cigars. Passing out cigars after the birth of a baby is in effect yelling, "See what a man I am? I have produced a child."

Asking a woman if she minds if he smokes a cigar is ridiculous. He knows he is going to stink up the place. He just wants her to be sure to see his masculinity symbol.

Beer

Men who stopped off for a few with the boys after work on the construction job drank the brand that centered its campaign on heavy-duty workmen. When the campaign changed to show people in dinner jackets drinking the brand, the construction workers complained that it didn't taste good anymore, that it had changed.

Wine

Wine sales were down a few years ago because of the psychological fear people had of serving the wrong wine with the wrong dinner. The wine companies came out with the "wine right for all occasions, all meals" campaign, and sales skyrocketed.

Buying a Dress

The average time it takes for a woman to buy a dress is ninety minutes.
Only 20 percent of women will buy the dress they really want. The one they just love they will pass over for the one that is "just right for their complexion" (60 percent) or the one that is in style (40 percent).

Appliances

You don't tell a housewife that by using this washer/dryer, she will have more time to play bridge or the like. She already feels guilty about not working as hard as her mother. You tell her she will be free to spend more time with her children and to be a good mother and wife.

Grocery Shopping

Women buy 35 percent more than they intended to buy, and men buy even more. A woman helped in the store will buy less than a woman left alone. She is embarrassed that she doesn't know more about food preparation, nutrition, and so on.

Soap

People with body odor secretly don't want to give it up; they see it as a defense mechanism against people. The soaps that promise to get rid of body odor do well only with extroverts or with introverts who long to be extroverts.

Airline Travel

Some years ago American Airlines became disturbed by the fact that many of its passengers flew only when it was imperative. The line hired a conventional research firm to find out why people didn't fly more often. The answer? They were afraid of dying. A great deal of money was spent to point out how safe flying was; the campaign had no results. Then an industrial psychologist was called in. He went into the problem in depth and even used projective tests that allowed potential travelers to imagine themselves involved in an air crash and being killed. His investigation showed that the primary thought in a man's mind at such times was not fear of his own death but, rather, how his family would receive the news. The researcher concluded that these men feared death less than their wives saying, "The darned fool. He should have gone by train." The airline took this diagnosis seriously and began aiming its campaign more at the "little woman" to persuade her that her husband would get home to her faster by flying and to get her in the air through family flying plans. In this way, the man was taken off the spot through the symbols of family-approved flying.

A Sample Parents' Bill of Rights

We have a right to expect from our teenagers:

1. temperance
2. frugality
3. honesty
4. frankness
5. trust
6. chastity
7. humility
8. industry
9. sincerity
10. a measure of privacy
11. keeping family affairs in the family
12. an effort to understand the parents' point of view
13. doing the best possible with the educational opportunity presented
14. a contribution to family activities
15. a pleasing attitude
16. sharing in family goals
17. practicing good manners that have been taught
18. being an asset, not a liability, in home responsibilities
19. honor
20. demonstrations of love and affection
21. obedience
22. appreciation
23. patience to hear us out before going off on a tangent
24. respect at least equal to that given to those outside the home
25. an understanding and practice of good religious and ethical training
26. an understanding of democratic principles and procedures (the degrees of freedom and the veto provision of every government, for example)

A Sample Students' Bill of Rights

We have a right to expect from our parents:

1. a degree of privacy
2. honesty
3. frankness
4. a genuine keen interest in our activities
5. an acceptance of our friends, an explanation of their disapproval
6. a free choice of religion
7. keeping family affairs in the family
8. teaching of responsibility
9. a happy marriage and family relationship
10. a decent example
11. trust
12. affection and love beyond doubt (nonpartiality)
13. proper sex education (knowledge and attitudes)
14. the essentials of life (food, shelter, clothing, and the like)
15. a gradual cutting of apron strings
16. sympathetic understanding of the teenagers' point of view
17. democratic practices and procedures (sharing personal and family decisions)
18. respect for individuality
19. encouragement for education
20. family activities
21. a pleasing attitude (attention to our troubles, keeping communication channels open)
22. training and practice in manners
23. ambition with and for us in achieving goals
24. a feeling of being an asset, not a liability
25. a right to choose own occupation
26. prompt attention to illness

27. religious and ethical training and practice
28. a feeling of security
29. wise counsel and guidance
30. brothers and/or sisters (?????)

How to Ruin Your Children

1. Give them everything they want. Teach them that the world owes them a living.

2. Laugh when they use bad words. Show them you think their use of such words is cute.

3. Never give spiritual training. Let children decide upon a faith for themselves when they grow up.

4. Avoid the use of the word "wrong." Otherwise, children may develop a guilt complex.

5. Pick up after them. Do everything for them. Give them experience in shirking responsibility.

6. Let them read anything. Let their minds feast on garbage.

7. Quarrel frequently in front of the children. Then they won't be shocked when the home breaks up.

8. Give them all the money they want.

9. Satisfy their cravings for drink, food, and comfort.

10. Take their sides against neighbors, teachers, and policemen.

11. Apologize for yourself when they get into trouble.

12. Prepare for a life of grief. You are likely to have it.

What the Child Learns

IF A CHILD LIVES WITH:	THE CHILD LEARNS:
criticism	to condemn
hostility	to fight
fear	to be apprehensive
pity	to be sorry for himself
jealousy	to feel resentment and/or suspicion
encouragement	to be confident
tolerance	to be patient
praise	to be appreciative
acceptance	to love
approval	to like himself
recognition	to have a goal
fairness	what justice is
honesty	what truth is
security	to have faith in himself
friendliness	that the world is a nice place in which to live

Reach Quiz

STRATEGY 142

How well are you and your son or daughter communicating? Write down the answers to the questions you want to answer. Then, ask your son or daughter to take the quiz. Your child will have to turn some parts of some questions around. For instance, he or she would reword question 7 from "Does your child think he or she gets enough allowance?" to "Do you think you get enough allowance?" Share your answers with each other. See if what you think your child feels is really how your child feels. See how well the two of you are connecting.

1. When was the last time you and your child had a serious discussion? What was it about?

2. When your family sets out to have just plain fun, what kinds of things do you do? go to a movie? go for a ride? throw a party? go to a club, school, or church gathering? sit around the living room and make up games? How do you decide what you all want to do? Do you plan such a time, or does it just happen? Do you think everybody in the family enjoys it, or feels *obligated* to enjoy it?

3. Can you tell, without your child's telling you, when he or she is feeling angry? happy? proud? guilty? sad? afraid? Can you tell how you express those feelings? Do you feel that you or the other people in your family are embarrassed to express certain feelings? Do you think that your child feels that you or other family members are embarrassed to express certain feelings? If certain feelings are hidden, do you think you can talk about them?

4. If you could change your child's appearance in any way, what would you do? cut his or her hair? throw away his or her tie-dyed jeans? Ask him or her to stand straighter? What do you think your child would like to change in his or her own appearance? What do you think your child would like to change in your appearance?

5. Do you think your child feels overdisciplined? underdisciplined? just about right? How was the discipline pattern established in your house? Did you set the rules? Did you and your child work them out together? Or do the rules depend upon the situation?

6. How do you feel about your child's friends? Do you like them, or not? Which ones don't you like, and why? How do you think your child feels about your friends?

7. Does your child's allowance depend on what he or she does around the house? If so, do you think your child is satisfied with his or her allowance? What do you think your child does with his or her money?

8. How do you organize the work to be done around the house? Does everybody share it? Does one person assign it? Do you do the work together? Is it fun, or is it something you hurry through so you can go out and have fun?

9. You've worked very late for about two weeks in a row. All you can think of tonight is a good, long sleep. But your child reminds you that it's the night of the Little League championship game. Or you get a surprise bonus vacation but it must be taken while your child is still in school. What do you do? How does your family handle a legitimate conflict of interests? Do you compromise? Does the one with the most desperate need have it his or her way? Does the one who gets his or her way promise to make up for it in the future?

10. What do you think your child really wants to do when he or she starts a career? Do you approve? Would you approve of anything your child wanted to be? a circus roustabout? a nuclear physicist? a poet? What do you think your child thinks of your career?

11. Aside from career goals, what do you think are your child's real interests? Are they anything like yours? Do you approve of them? Do you allow your child to follow personal interests freely, or do you sometimes try to direct your child's interests? Is your child willing, eager, or reluctant to try your suggestions?

12. Do you think your child knows what your real interests are? What do you think your child thinks about your interests? Do you think that he or she approves of them?

13. Do you think your child has any special talents? What are they? What do you think your child feels his or her special talents to be? What do you think your child feels your special talents to be?

14. Your child wakes you up at 3:00 in the morning and wants to talk. Do you get up or tell your child you'll talk tomorrow? Are you annoyed, happy that the child feels free enough with you to impose on your sleep, or worried? What do you think your child would do if you woke him or her at 3:00 in the morning? How do you think he or she would feel?

15. What two things do you think make your child feel most angry? happiest? proudest? guiltiest? saddest? most afraid? What do you think your child thinks provokes these feelings in you?

Shipwreck![6]

[6]Reprinted by permission from *Scholastic Search,* © 1973 by Scholastic Magazines, Inc.

STRATEGY 180

Shipwreck is a game of the future. Your whole class is in the game. After playing Shipwreck, you will know more abut how people build a society. A society is a group of people who live and work together. You will learn why governments are needed. You will learn why money is printed and why banks are started. You will learn how people decide what jobs to do. You will have to make the laws for your group. And you will have to decide what to do about people who break the law. At the end of the game, you will have to decide whether or not to go to war! Can you build your own society? Before you start, you've got to get some background. Choose someone in your class to read the important fact sheet.

FACT SHEET

In the year 2000, the world ran out of oil and gasoline. All cars, trucks, trains, and planes could not move. All factories had to close down. Suddenly, millions of people all over the world were without work. With no work, they earned no money. Soon there were millions of hungry people. They began fighting for every scrap of food. Civil wars broke out in every nation.

The U.S. decided to get a group of students together and take them out of the country by ship. The U.S. wanted to save their lives.

For a while, the ship carrying the students sailed smoothly. But a few weeks later, a storm came up. The ship hit a large sandbar. It started to sink. The students got into lifeboats. They swam to an island.

When they got to the island, the students listened to their transistor radios. They learned that their homes had been destroyed. They learned that hunger and disease were spreading all over the world. They decided to spend the next 10 to 15 years on the island. They named the island *Terra*.

The students are the only people on Terra. The island is very beautiful. There are plenty of coconuts, bananas, and other fresh fruits to eat. There are fish in the waters to catch. There is fresh water to drink in the hills. The average temperature is 80 degrees.

CAN *YOU* LIVE ON TERRA?

Suppose that the students in your class are the young people on Terra. You have escaped the hunger, disease, and violence of the world. But you have a lot of work to do if you want to survive on Terra.

Every day brings a new problem. So this game is divided into days. You may want to divide your class into groups. Then each group can work on a different problem. Or, you may want to choose people to act out the parts of the young people on Terra. Then your entire class can listen and decide how to solve the problems.

Remember, there are no right or wrong answers. Only *you* can decide the rules you will live by on Terra.

DAY 1

Larry: Now that we are all together, we must choose a leader. We need someone to make decisions. We need someone to tell us what to do so that we don't all die here.

Sarah: But, Larry, we know what we have to do. We know we all have to work together to build homes, find food, and everything. We don't need a leader to tell us that.

Sam: We need a leader who can tell each one of us what our job will be. We won't get anything done without a leader.

Alice: We are all the same here on Terra. We don't want some people to be leaders and some people to be followers. Why don't we choose a new leader every day, or every week? That way, one person won't get more powerful than everyone else.

Sarah: I still say we don't need a leader at all. Why don't we just choose someone to be in charge of building homes. And someone else to be in charge of building a fire. And someone else to be in charge of getting food.

Larry: That's no good. I want to be leader. Anyone who wants me to be the leader, follow me!

This is a serious problem. Do you need a leader or not? You must decide. Make two lists. On one list, write down all the reasons you can think of for having a leader. On the other list, write down all the reasons for not having a leader. If your class decides you need a leader, then you must decide how to choose one. Your class must solve this problem as quickly as they can!

DAY 2

There is much work to do to keep your group together-and to stay alive. For example, some sort of shelter must be built. What other jobs must be done during your first few months on Terra? Make a list of all the jobs you can think of.

DAY 3

Sam: I am marking off this part of the beach. This is my land.

Larry: If you're taking part of the beach, I want that hill over there. I claim it. It's mine.

Alice: Wait a minute! Stop! We all own this whole island together. Let's not divide it up. There isn't enough good land to give everyone an equal share. So some people won't get any land at all. That will only lead to fights and trouble!

Sam: No. I want my own property. I may have kids some day. I want something I can call mine. Something I can be proud of!

Sarah: But the whole island is yours. Let's all enjoy it together.

You must decide what to do about property. Should everyone own the entire island together? Should you divide it up? If you do divide it up, some people will not get good land. Where will they live? Will they have to work someone else's land in exchange for living on it? Will they have to pay rent for land they use? You must decide how to solve this problem.

DAY 4

Sarah: Mmm, those oranges you picked look great, Larry. Can I have one?

Larry: I'll trade you an orange for one of those coconuts you pulled down.

Sarah: Are you kidding? One coconut is worth at least four oranges!

Larry: I'll give you two oranges for one—no more.

Bob: Does anyone want this rope I made? I'll take 10 coconuts for it.

Sarah: Ten coconuts? How about five coconuts and these bowls I made?

Bob: Bowls? I don't want bowls. I want coconuts.

Larry: You know what we need? We need money. It's too hard to trade stuff all the time.

Sarah: Oh, no! I'm glad we don't have to worry about money on Terra.

Bob: We *have* to have money, Sarah. If I make a rope, I should be paid for it. Then I'd have the money to buy your bowls.

Sarah: No. We all work for the fun of it—and because we *have* to. We don't need money as a reward. We will share everything.

Larry: I don't agree. Money isn't a reward. It's a way to help us trade the things we grow and make. The person who works the hardest should get the most money. It's only fair. If we share everything, some people won't work at all.

Sam: Money only leads to stealing. We don't want rich people and poor people on Terra. We all want to be the same.

Ben: That's stupid, Sam. If we don't have money, people will just steal the goods we grow and make. We need money. I won't work unless I get paid for it.

You must decide what to do about this problem. Should you have money or not? What problems would you have with money? What problems do you have without money? If you decide to have money, who will get the money? Will everyone get the same amount each week? What will you use for money? You must decide.

DAY 5

Five members of your group disagree with the decision you made about money. They say they will not go along with your decision. You must decide what to do about them. Should they be punished? Should they be put in prison? Should you just leave them alone? You must decide.

DAY 6

Alice: Someone has been leaving banana peels by the main camp fire. We need a law against people who litter.

Bob: That's right. We don't want pollution on Terra. We need a law against littering.

Sarah: Are you crazy? We don't want any laws like that. We don't want any laws at all. Once you start making laws, you can't stop. First thing you know, everything is against the law.

Alice: We have to have laws. But the problem is, how will we enforce the law. Maybe we need to assign some people to be police.

Benny: No, we don't need police. Not on Terra. If we draw up a list of laws, we will all obey them. Those who don't obey the laws will be punished by all of us.

Sarah: Maybe we just need laws about important crimes — like murder or stealing. Maybe we should just have a few laws against big crimes like those.

Now you must solve this problem. Do you need laws or not? If so, what laws? Who will make the laws? How will you enforce the laws? You must decide. After you decide, act out what happens next to the litterers.

DAY 7

You have been on Terra for nearly a year. Everything has been going smoothly. Then one day, three boats appear. A group of 20 people have come to Terra. You greet them.

"We are going to live on Terra," their leader says. "But we do not wish to live with your group. We want to stay by ourselves. We can live in peace. Just give us half of the island."

"No," you say. "We don't think there should be two groups on Terra. We welcome you. But you must live and work with us. We have worked hard here. We don't want to give away half of our island. Stay with us."

"No," their leader says. "We don't want to be with you. If you do not give us half of Terra, we will fight you for it."

You must solve this problem. Do you give them half of Terra? Do you try to talk them into staying with you? Do you have a summit meeting — your leader talking to their leader? Or do you go to war to keep them from taking half the island? You must decide. Then act out what happens next.

Body Ritual among the Nacirema[7]

STRATEGY 181

The anthropologist has become so familiar with the diversity of ways in which different peoples behave in similar situations that he is not apt to be surprised by even the most exotic customs. In fact, if all the logically possible combinations of behavior have not been found somewhere in the world, he is apt to suspect that they must be present in some yet undescribed tribe. This point has, in fact, been expressed with respect to clan organization by Mardock (1949:71). In this light, the magical belief and practices of the Nacirema present such unusual aspects that it seems desirable to describe them as an example of the extremes to which human behavior can go.

Professor Linton first brought the ritual of the Nacirema to the attention of anthropologists twenty years ago (1936:326), but the culture of this people is still very poorly understood. They are a North American group living in the territory between the Canadian Cree, the Yaqui and Tarahumare of Mexico, and the Carab and Arawak of the Antilles.

Nacirema culture is characterized by a highly developed market economy which has evolved in a rich natural habitat. While much of the people's time is devoted to economic pursuits, a large part of the fruits of these labors and a considerable portion of the day is spent in ritual activity. The focus of this activity is the human body, the appearance and health of which loom as a dominant concern in the ethos of the people. While such a concern is certainly not usual, its ceremonial aspects and associated philosophy are unique.

The fundamental beliefs underlying the whole system appear to be that the human body is ugly and that its natural tendency is to debility and disease. Incarnated in such a body, man's only hope is to avert these characteristics through the use of shrines devoted to this

---

[7]Reproduced by permission of the American Anthropological Association from the *American Anthropologist,* 58 (3), 1956.

purpose. The more powerful individuals in the society have several shrines in their houses and, in fact, the opulence of a house is often referred to in terms of the number of such ritual centers it possesses. Most houses are of wattle and daub construction; the shrine rooms of the more wealthy are walled with stone. Poorer families imitate the rich by applying pottery placques to their shrine walls.

While each family has at least one such shrine, the rituals associated with it are not family ceremonies, but are private and secret. The rites are normally only discussed with children, and then only during the period when they are being initiated into these mysteries. I was able, however, to establish sufficient rapport with the natives to examine these shrines and to have the ritual described to me.

The focal point of the shrine is a box or chest which is built into the wall. In this chest are kept the many charms and magical potions without which no native believes he would or could live. These preparations are secured from a variety of specialized practitioners. The most powerful of these are the medicine men, whose assistance must be rewarded with substantial gifts. However, the medicine men do not provide the curative potions for their clients, but decide what the ingredients should be and then write them down in a secret language. This writing is understood only by the medicine men and by the herbalists who, for another gift, provide the required charm.

The charm is not disposed of after it has served its purpose, but is placed in the charm box of the household shrine. As these magical materials are specific for certain ills, and the real or imagined maladies of the people are many, the charm box is usually full to overflowing. The magical packets are so numerous tha people forget what their purposes were and fear to use them again. While the natives are very vague on this point, we can only assume that the idea in retaining all the old magical materials is that their presence in the charm box, before which the body rituals are conducted, will in some way protect the worshipper.

Beneath the charm box is a small font. Each day every member of the family, in succession, enters the shrine room, bows his head before the charm box, mingles different sorts of holy water in the font, and proceeds with a brief rite of ablution. The holy waters are secured from the Water Temple of the community, where the priests conduct elaborate ceremonies to make the liquid ritually pure.

In the hierarchy of magical practitioners, and below the medicine men in prestige, are specialists whose designation is best translated "holy-mouth men." The Nacirema have almost pathological horror of and fascination with the mouth, the condition of which is believed to have a supernatural influence on all social relationships. Were it not for the rituals of the mouth, they believe that their teeth would fall out, their gums bleed, their jaws shrink, their friends desert them, and their lovers reject them. They also believe that a strong relationship exists between oral and moral characteristics. For example, there is a ritual ablution of the mouth for children which is supposed to improve their moral fiber.

The daily body ritual performed by everyone includes a mouth-rite. Despite the fact that these people are so punctilious about the care of the mouth, this rite involves a practice which strikes the uninitiated stranger as revolting. It was reported to me that the ritual consists of inserting small hog hairs into the mouth, along with certain magical powders, and then moving the bundle in a highly formalized series of gestures.

In addition to the private mouth-rite, the people seek out a holy-mouth man once or twice a year. These practitioners have an impressive set of paraphernalia, consisting of a variety of augers, awls, probes, and prods. The use of these objects in the exorcism of the evil of the mouth involves almost unbelievable ritual torture of the clients. The holy-mouth man opens the client's mouth and, using the above-mentioned tools, enlarges any holes which decay may have created in the teeth. Magical materials are put into these holes. If there are no naturally occurring holes in the teeth, large sections of one or more teeth are gouged out so that the supernatural substance can be applied. In the client's view, the purpose of these ministrations is to arrest decay and to draw friends. The extremely sacred and traditional character of the rite is evident in the fact that the natives return to the holy-mouth man year after year, despite the fact that their teeth continue to decay.

It is to be hoped that, when a thorough study of the Nacirema is made, there will be careful inquiry into the personality structure of these people. One has but to watch the gleam in the eye of a holy-mouth man, as he jabs an awl into an exposed nerve, to suspect that a certain amount of sadism is involved. If this can be established very interesting patterns emerge, for most of the population shows definite masochistic tendencies. It was to these that Professor Linton referred in discussing a distinctive part of the daily body-ritual which is performed only by the men. This part of the rite involved scraping and lacerating the surface of the face with a sharp instrument. Special women's rites are performed only four times during each lunar month, but what they lack in frequency is made up in barbarity. As part of this ceremony, women bake their heads in small ovens for about an hour.

The theoretically interesting point is that what seems to be a preponderantly masochistic people have developed sadistic specialties.

The medicine men have an interesting and imposing temple, or latipsoh, in every community of any size. The more elaborate ceremonies required to treat very sick patients can only be performed at this temple. These ceremonies involve not only the thaumaturge but a permanent group of vestal maidens who move about the temple chambers in distinctive costumes and headdress.

The latipsoh ceremonies are so harsh that it is phenomenal that a fair proportion of the really sick natives who enter ever recover. Small children whose indoctrination is still incomplete have been known to resist attempts to be taken to the temple because "that is where you go to die." Despite this fact, sick adults are not only willing but eager to undergo the protracted ritual purification, if they can afford to do so. No matter how ill the supplicant or how grave the emergency, the guardians of many temples will not admit a client if he cannot give a rich gift to the custodian. Even after one has gained admissions and survived the ceremonies the guardians will not permit the neophyte to leave until he makes still another gift.

The supplicant entering the temple is first stripped of all his or her clothes. In everyday life the Nacirema avoids exposure of his body and its natural functions. Bathing and excretory acts are performed only in the secrecy of the household shrine, where they are ritualized as part of the body-rites. Psychological shock results from the fact that body secrecy is suddenly lost upon entry into the latipsoh. A man, whose own wife has never seen him in an excretory act, suddenly finds himself naked and assisted by a vestal maiden while he performs his natural functions into a sacred vessel. This sort of ceremonial treatment is necessitated by the fact that the excrements are used by a divinor to ascertain the course and nature of the client's sickness. Female clients, on the other hand, find their naked bodies are subjected to the scrutiny, manipulation, and probing of the medicine men.

Few supplicants in the temple are well enough to do anything but lie on their backs on the hard beds. The daily ceremonies, like the rites, involve discomfort and torture. With ritual precision, the vestals awaken their miserable charges each dawn and roll them about on their bed of pain while performing ablutions in the formal movements of which the maidens are highly trained. At other times they insert magical viands in the supplicant's mouth or force him to eat substances which are supposed to be healing. From time to time, the medicine men come to their clients and jab magically treated needles into their flesh. The fact that these temple ceremonies may not cure, and may even kill, the neophyte in no way decreases the people's faith in the medicine men.

There remains one other kind of practitioner, known as a "listener." This witch doctor has the power to exorcise the devils that lodge in the heads of people who have been bewitched. The Nacirema believe that parents bewitch their children. Mothers are particularly suspected of putting a curse on children while teaching them the secret body rituals. The counter-magic of the witch doctor is unusual in its lack of ritual. The patient simply tells the listener all his troubles and fears, beginning with the earliest difficulties he can remember. The memory displayed by the Nacirema in these exorcism sessions is truly remarkable. It is not uncommon for the patient to bemoan the rejection he felt upon being weaned as a babe, and a few individuals even see their troubles going to the effect of their own birth.

In conclusion, mention must be made of certain practices which have their base in native esthetics but which depend upon the persuasive aversion to the natural body and its functions. There are ritual fasts to make fat people thin and ceremonial feasts to make thin people fat. Still other rites are used to make women's breasts larger if they are small, and smaller if they are large. General dissatisfaction with breast shape is symbolized in the fact that the ideal form is virtually outside the range of human variation. A few women afflicted with almost inhuman-type mammary development are so idolized that they make a handsome living by simply going from village to village and permitting the natives to stare at them for a fee.

Reference has already been made to the fact that excretory functions are ritualized, and relegated to secrecy. Natural reproductive functions are similarly distorted. Intercourse is taboo as a topic and scheduled as an act. Efforts are made to avoid pregnancy by the use of magical materials or by limiting intercourse to certain phases of the moon. Conception is actually very infrequent. When pregnant, women dress so as to hide their condition. Parturition takes place in secret, without friends or relatives to assist, and a majority of the women do not nurse their infants.

Our review of the ritual life of the Nacirema has certainly shown them to be a magic-ridden people. It is hard to understand how they have managed to exist so long under the burdens which they have imposed upon themselves. But even such exotic customs as these take on real meaning when they are viewed with the insight provided by Malinowski when he wrote "Looking from far and above, from our high places of safety in the developed civilization, it is easier to see all the crudity and irrelevance of magic. But without its power and guidance, early man could not have mastered his practical difficulties as he has done, nor could man have advanced to the highest stages of civilization."

Film Distributors

Catalogs are available from the film distributors listed below. The catalog offered by the University of Illinois is extremely useful; it is the most extensive and the films are the least expensive to rent.

Association Instructional Materials
25358 Cypress Avenue
Hayward, CA 94544

Audio Brandon Films
3868 Piedmont Avenue
Oakland, CA 94611

BFA Educational Media
2211 Michigan Avenue
Santa Monica, CA 90404

Contemporary/McGraw-Hill Films
Sales Service Department
1221 Avenue of the Americas
New York, NY 10020

Creative Film Society
7237 Canby Avenue
Reseda, CA 91335

Extension Media Center
University of California
Berkeley, CA 94720

Impact Films
144 Bleecker Street
New York, NY 10012

Instructional Communication Center
Media Library
State University of New York
  at Buffalo
22 Foster Avenue
Buffalo, NY 14214

Montana State Audiovisual Library
Office of the Superintendent
  of Public Instruction
Helena, MT 59601

National Audiovisual Center
National Archives and Records
  Service
General Services Administration
Washington, DC 20409

Pyramid Film
Box 1048
Santa Monica, CA 90406

Twyman Films
329 Salem Avenue
Dayton, OH 45401

University of Illinois Visual Aids
  Service
Division University Extension
University of Illinois
Champaign, IL 61820

University of Southern California
Division of Cinema
Film Distribution Section
University Park
Los Angeles, CA 90007

Manufacturers of Simulation Games

The best source for simulation games is Interact, although other companies have produced some very worthwhile products. All the companies listed below provide catalogs.

ABT Associates, Inc.
4 Concord Lane
Cambridge, MA 02138

American Institute for Research
P.O. Box 1113
Palo Alto, CA 94302

Center for Educational Services
and Research
845 Fox Meadow Road
Yorktown Heights, NY 10598

Educational Development Center
55 Chapel Street
Newton, MA 02158

Educational Development Center
15 Mifflin Place
Cambridge, MA 02138

Educational Manpower, Inc.
P.O. Box 4272-B
Madison, WI 53711

Entelek, Inc.
42 Pleasant Street
Newburyport, MA 01950

4H Foundation
7100 Connecticut Avenue, NW
Washington, DC 20015

Greenhaven Press, Inc.
P.O. Box 831
Anoka, MN 55305

Interact
P.O. Box 262
Lakeside, CA 92040

Joint Council on Economic
Education
1212 Avenue of the Americas
New York, NY 10036

Simile II
P.O. Box 910
Del Mar, CA 55303

Social Studies School Service
10000 Culver Boulevard
Culver City, CA 90230

Systems Gaming Associates
Triphammer Road
Ithaca, NY 14850

Wellesley School Curriculum Center
12 Seaward Road
Wellesley Hills, MA 02181

Western Publishing, Inc.
850 Third Avenue
New York, NY 10022

World Law Fund
11 West 42nd Street
New York, NY 10036

Publishers of Educational Materials

The publishers listed below offer everything from old photographs to cassette tapes. All supply brochures describing materials they have available in the social-studies area.

Allyn and Bacon, Inc.
Ralston Park
Belmont, CA 94002

Allyn and Bacon, Inc.
Longwood Division
Link Drive
Rockleigh, NJ 07647

Argus Communications
7440 Natchez Avenue
Niles, IL 60648

Audio Visual Narrative Arts, Inc.
P.O. Box 398
Pleasantville, NY 10570

Barron's Educational Series, Inc.
113 Crossways Park Drive
Woodbury, NY 11797

Cambridge Book Company
488 Madison Avenue
New York, NY 10022

Carmen Educational Assoc., Inc.
P.O. Box 205
Youngstown, NY 14174

Charles E. Merrill Publishing Co.
1300 Alum Creek Drive
Columbus, OH 43216

Civic Education Service
1725 K Street NW, Suite 1009
Washington, DC 20006

Corner House Publishers
Green River Road
Williamstown, MA 01267

Creative Lessons, U.S.A.
P.O. Box 191
Elmira, NY 14902

Curriculum Innovations, Inc.
501 Lake Forest Avenue
Highwood, IL 60040

Documentary Photo Aids
P.O. Box 956
Mt. Dora, FL 32757

Doubleday Multimedia
P.O. Box 11607
Santa Ana, CA 92705

Dow Jones Reprint Service
Educational Service Bureau
P.O. Box 300
Princeton, NJ 08540

Educational Audio Visual, Inc.
Pleasantville, NY 10570

Educational Record Sales
157 Chambers Street
New York, NY 10007

Educational Resources Center
Opt
855 Broadway
Boulder, CO 80302

Forum for Contemporary History
812 Anacapa Street
Santa Barbara, CA 93101

Foundation for Change
1841 Broadway
New York, NY 10023

Franciscan Communication Center
1229 South Santee Street
Los Angeles, CA 90015

General Media Corporation
P.O. Box 126
900 Olive Way
Monmouth, OR 97361

Greenhaven Press
P.O. Box 831
Anoka, MN 55303

Guidance Associates
757 Third Avenue
New York, NY 10017

Harcourt Brace Jovanovich
757 3rd Avenue
New York, NY 10017

Harper and Row Publishers, Inc.
Media Dept. 3-A
10 East 53rd Street
New York, NY 10022

Harper and Row Publishers, Inc.
Keystone Industrial Park
Scranton, PA 18512

Holt, Rinehart and Winston, Inc.
Valley Road
Crocker Park
Brisbane, CA 94005

Houghton Mifflin
777 California Avenue
Palo Alto, CA 94303

Inor Publishing Co.
Roxbury Boulevard
Sweet Springs, MO 65351

Inquiry Audio-Visual
1754 West Farragut Avenue
Chicago, IL 60640

J. Weston Walch, Publisher
Portland, ME 04104

Key Publications
P.O. Box 293B
Wheeling, IL 60090

Lansford Publishing Company
P.O. Box 8711
San Jose, CA 95155

McDougal, Littell and Company
P.O. Box 1667-B
Evanston, IL 60204

Multi-Media Production, Inc.
P.O. Box 5097
Stanford, CA 94305

National Geographic Society
Dept. 1231
P.O. Box 1640
Washington, DC 20013

North Country Publications
Terrace Heights
Winona, MN 55987

Research Media, Inc.
4 Midland Avenue
Kicksville, NY 11801

Scholastic Magazines
902 Sylvan Avenue
Englewood Cliffs, NJ 07632

Scott Education
385 Lower Westfield Road
Holyoke, MA 01040

Scott, Foresman and Co.
855 California Ave.
Palo Alto, CA 94304

Simon and Schuster, Inc.
1 West 39th Street
New York, NY 10018

Social Studies School Service
10000 Culver Boulevard, Dept 48
Culver City, CA 90230

Sunburst Communications
Executive Offices
Pound Ridge, NY 10576

Teacher's Guide to Television
P.O. Box 564
Lenox Hill Station
New York, NY 10021

The Center for Cassette Studies
8110 Webb Avenue
North Hollywood, CA 91605

The Perfection Form Company
P.O. Box 147
Logan, IA 51546

T. S. Denison and Co.
5100 West 82nd Street
Minneapolis, MN 55437

United Settlement Supply
P.O. Box 907 Ansonia Station
New York, NY 10023

United States History Society, Inc.
5425 West Fargo
Skokie, IL 60076

VEC, Inc.
P.O. Box 52
Madison, WI 53701

Bibliography

The works mentioned were instrumental in the preparation of this book. Books are recommended on the basis of their usability.

Alschuler, Alfred, Diane Tabor, and James McIntrye, *Teaching Achievement Motivation*. Middletown, Conn.: Education Ventures, 1971.

Ardrey, Robert, *The Territorial Imperative*. New York: Dell, 1966.

Bach, Richard, *Jonathan Livingston Seagull*. New York: Avon Books, 1970.

Barzun, Jacques, *Teacher in America*. Boston: Little, Brown and Company, 1944.

Biehler, Robert, *Psychology Applied to Teaching*. Palo Alto, Calif.: Houghton Mifflin Company, 1974.

Conant, James, *The American High School Today*. New York: Signet Books, 1959.

Cox, Donald, *The City as a Schoolhouse*. Valley Forge, Pa.: Judson Press, 1972.

Daniels, Steven, *How 2 Gerbils, 20 Goldfish, 200 Games and 2,000 Books and I Taught Them to Read*. Philadelphia: Westminster Press, 1971.

de Saint Exupery, Antoine, *The Little Prince*. New York: Harcourt Brace Jovanovich, 1943.

Dewey, John, *Experience and Education*. New York: Collier Books, 1938.

Elizabeth Cleaver Street School People, *Starting Your Own High School*. New York: Vintage Books, 1972.

Fromm, Erich, *The Art of Loving*. New York: Harper Colophon Books, 1956.

Ginandes, Shepard, *The School We Have*. New York: Delacorte Press, 1973.

Glasser, William, *Schools Without Failure*. New York: Harper & Row, 1969.

Greer, Mary, and Bonnie Rubinstein, *Will the Real Teacher Please Stand Up: A Primer in Humanistic Education*. Pacific Palisades, Calif.: Goodyear Publishing, 1972.

Gross, Beatrice, and Ronald Gross, editors, *Radical School Reform*. New York: Simon & Schuster, 1969.

Holt, John, *How Children Fail.* New York: Dell, 1964.

————, *What Do I Do Monday?* New York: Dell, 1970.

Kellum, David, *The Social Studies: Myths and Realities.* New York: Sheed & Ward, 1969.

Kirschenbaum, Howard, Sidney Simon, and Rodney Napier, *Wad-Ja-Get?* New York: Hart, 1971.

Kohl, Herbert, *Half the House.* New York: Bantam Books, 1974.

————, *The Open Classroom.* New York: Vintage, 1969.

Kozol, Jonathan, *Free Schools.* Boston: Houghton Mifflin, 1972.

Lair, Jess, *I Ain't Much Baby—But I'm All I've Got.* Garden City, N.Y.: Doubleday, 1972.

Leonard, George, *Education and Ecstasy.* New York: Dell, 1968.

————, *Ultimate Athlete.* New York: Viking Press, 1974.

Lewis, Harold, and Howard Streitfeld, *Growth Games.* New York: Bantam Books, 1971.

Mager, Robert F., *Preparing Instructional Objectives.* Second Edition, Belmont, Calif.: Fearon-Pitman, 1975.

Maltz, Maxwell, *Psycho-Cybernetics.* New York: Prentice-Hall, 1960.

Mann, John, *Learning to Be.* New York: Macmillan, 1972.

Martin, John, and Charles Harrison, *Free to Learn.* Englewood Cliffs, N.J.: Prentice Hall, 1972.

Mead, Margaret, *Culture and Commitment.* New York: Doubleday, 1970.

Michener, James, *Sports in America.* New York, Random House, 1976.

Perlstein, Marcia, editor, *Flowers Can Even Bloom in Schools.* Sunnyvale, Calif.: Westinghouse Learning Press, 1974.

Postman, Neil, and Charles Weingartner, *Teaching As a Subversive Activity.* New York: Delacorte Press, 1969.

————, *The School Book.* New York: Delacorte Press, 1973.

————, *The Soft Revolution.* New York: Dell, 1971.

Reich, Charles, *The Greening of America.* New York: Random House, 1970.

Reimer, Everett, *School Is Dead.* Garden City, N.Y.. Doubleday, 1970.

Roszak, Theodore, *The Making of a Counter Culture.* Garden City, N.Y.: Doubleday, 1968.

Rubin, David, *The Rights of Teachers.* New York: Avon Books, 1972.

Schultz, William, *Joy*. New York: Grove Press, 1971.

Scott, John, *Teaching for a Change*. New York: Bantam Books, 1972.

Shostrom, Everett, *Man and Manipulator*. New York: Bantam Books, 1967.

Shrank, Jeffrey, *Teaching Human Beings: 101 Subversive Activities for the Classroom*. Boston: Beacon Press, 1972.

Silberman, Charles, *Crisis in the Classroom*. New York: Random House, 1970.

Simon, Sidney, and Jay Clark, *Beginning Values Clarification*. San Diego, Calif.: Pennant Press, 1975.

Simon, Sidney, Leland Howe, and Howard Kirschenbaum, *Values Clarification*. New York: Hart Publishing, 1972.

Taylor, John, and Rex Walford, *Simulation in the Classroom*. Middlesex, England: Penquin Books, 1972.

Toffler, Alvin, *Future Shock*. New York: Bantam Books, 1970.